LAURA ASHLEY

Decorating with Fabric

LAURA ASHLEY

Decorating with Fabric

A ROOM-BY-ROOM GUIDE TO HOME DECORATING

LORRIE MACK AND DIANA LODGE

Special Photography by Tim Imrie

CROWN TRADE PAPERBACKS
NEW YORK

First published in the United Kingdom in 1995 by Ebury Press
Random House, 20 Vauxhall Bridge Road, London SW1V 2SA

Published by Crown Publishers, Inc., 201 East 50th Street, New York, New York 10022. Member
of the Crown Publishing Group.

Random House, Inc. New York, Toronto, London, Sydney, Auckland

CROWN TRADE PAPERBACKS and colophon are trademarks of Crown Publishers, Inc.

Manufactured in Great Britain by Butler and Tanner Ltd, Frome, Somerset

Library of Congress cataloging-in-publication data is available on request

Project Editor: Cindy Richards
Edited by Alison Wormleighton
Designed by Christine Wood
Special photography by Tim Imrie
Styling by Jacky Boase and Janie Jackson
Illustrations by Kate Simunek
Picture research by Kate Duffy

ISBN: 0-517-88229-9

10 9 8 7 6 5 4 3 2 1

First American Edition

Contents

Introduction

Decorating and accessorizing our homes has a higher profile than it used to have. Our awareness of interiors and interest in craftsmanship has heightened, encouraged by all the media publications and the large number of mainstream home-furnishing shops offering choice and services.

The notable difference today is in attention to detail, particularly in soft sewn furnishings. The extent to which new detail can update a room is astonishing. In this book you'll find all the distinguishing finishing touches and the know-how to transform your home. The projects range from stylish curtain treatments to smaller-scale accessories such as a tea cosy and a flanged cushion made from patterned tea towels.

Laura Ashley is somewhat of a pioneer in making elegant window treatments accessible to everyone. We were the first to launch a mail-order, made-to-measure blind and curtain service in 1982. Since then we have consistently brought exciting and fashionable products to the marketplace, and our expertise in design and preoccupation with comfort, quality and value for money make us a credible authority on soft furnishings.

The chapters are usefully arranged room by room. Each chapter opens with an inspirational photograph of an interior designed by us especially for the book. The text combines exciting ideas with practical advice, followed by step-by-step instructions for each project. With its unique combination of exclusive ideas and uncomplicated advice, this book will inspire you and give you the confidence to redecorate in the Laura Ashley style.

Emma Ashley

Providing both effective insulation and a decorative link with the country garden beyond, these blossom-strewn curtains draw neatly over an interesting stable door. The narrow pelmet (cornice) leaves enough room for clearance, and extends uninterrupted across a matching pair at the nearby window.

CHAPTER ONE

Colour, Texture & Pattern

M ost homes contain the same basic furniture – chairs, tables, beds, and various items for storage, from large dressers to small cabinets. The elements that infuse it with life, warmth, comfort, humanity, and the personality of its owners are textiles: an eclectic collection of curtains and blinds, upholstery and cushions, carpets and rugs, bedlinen and quilts, and stylish accessories like lampshades, tablecloths, and wall hangings. Some of these will have been installed as part of a general decorating project, some will have been received as gifts, and some will have been collected as decorative mementos of travels abroad. Whether your preference is for an elaborate period style or a more streamlined contemporary look, the tactile surface and graceful drape of cotton, linen, wool, or silk will always enhance it.

This assortment of plump and inviting cushions illustrates the variety of different furnishing textiles that can be used together successfully. Stripes, checks, florals and plain materials can all be utilized in combination, or individually, for both period and contemporary interiors.

FABRIC OF THE PAST

The ornamental and civilizing qualities of textiles have always been valued very highly. During the early Middle Ages, the need for landed aristocrats to keep a close eye on all their estates kept many large households on the move. Invariably, they carried with them all the furnishings that made everyday life as pleasant and luxurious as possible, and acted as a visual symbol of the family's wealth and position. These possessions were predominantly textiles: rich bed hangings, hand-woven tapestries to decorate the walls and provide insulation, animal skins and embroidered cushions to soften hard surfaces, and Oriental carpets to drape over tables and shelves.

When society became more stable, the continuing importance of domestic textiles was reflected in the exalted position held in trade of the "upholder"; from the middle of the fourteenth century, he was responsible for overseeing every type of soft furnishing, including the vital *passementerie*, or trimmings, which included everything from tassels and fringe to braid and lace. Acting in much the same way that interior decorators do today, he supervised all the other internal work such as gilding and carving as well. In addition, he valued the contents of a house after a death, dressed all the rooms and the family coach in elaborate black hangings, and then went on to act as undertaker. By the mid-nineteenth century, specialist funeral directors had taken on the undertaking responsibilities, and the upholder, who by then had become known as an upholsterer, was someone who made and fitted curtains, carpets, and hangings as well as stuffing and covering chairs, stools, and sofas.

The Victorian age was perhaps the heyday of domestic textiles. The fashion for extravagant use of fabric stemmed at least partly from the fact that the industrial revolution made it possible for dyed and printed cloth to be manufactured for the first time in large quantities, at more affordable prices. In today's world, more than a century later, improved technology, coupled with the survival of centuries-old traditional skills and techniques, has resulted in the availability of an enormous range of beautiful fabrics and stylish trimmings from all over the world.

The most unusual feature of this bedroom is the curtain hung against the wall to frame the bed. Its colour and pattern impart a solid, masculine feel to the room, yet the antique lace trimming and pink material around the bed do not look at all out of place. Note the use of a toning scarf to soften the lines of the otherwise plain mirror frame.

Toning, neutral shades have been used here to great effect, giving a feeling of space and calmness. The style is set by the natural floor covering and the white paintwork. Details such as the decoration on the cushion and the scalloped edge of the chair cover add interest without spoiling the understated look.

UNLIMITED OPTIONS

For many people, this almost unlimited choice is both inspiring and bewildering. If you feel confused, keep in mind that whether you're faced with choosing a single pair of curtains or the soft furnishings for a whole house, your task will be much easier and the result more successful if you follow a few simple guidelines.

In deciding on an overall look, make sure the one you choose is broadly in keeping with the architectural style of your home. Large, elaborately draped swags and pelmets (cornices) are ideal in a Georgian or Victorian room, but their grand proportions are usually unsuitable in a low-ceilinged cottage or a modest urban apartment. Similarly, dainty ruffles and narrow borders that look enchanting in a modest period dwelling can be completely overwhelmed by the large scale and solid structure of a barn or warehouse conversion.

When choosing colours, don't be afraid to follow your instincts. If you never wear green, you won't feel happy in a predominantly green room, no matter how fashionable a particular shade might be. If you've always loved yellow, use it to create warm, sunny surroundings that give you real pleasure and lift your spirits. If you like being surrounded by neutrals such as white, grey, and cream, don't worry that they could be boring – neutrals can make just as strong a statement as vibrant shades. On the other hand, there's no need to restrict yourself to safe, pale shades: instead of light yellow, you could try vibrant buttercup or deep ochre. Colours of the same value work best together – a navy sofa would look sensational with maroon, chestnut, or bottle green, while it could make curtains in a perfectly respectable pastel pink simply look faded and washed out.

In the same way, try creating bold and exciting effects by combining patterns in your own very personal way. Novices can ensure success by sticking to patterns which are the same approximate scale and mood; mix fresh, bright checked gingham with simple country florals; subtle *toiles de Jouy* with elegant Georgian stripes; or tiny geometric motifs with all-over textural designs. When you gain experience, try more adventurous combinations such as small prints with large checks.

USING THIS BOOK

The very fact that textiles are so diverse and versatile means they can either act as stylish accents to an existing scheme, or transform a room totally. This book sets out a collection of soft-furnishing projects that have all been chosen to provide the maximum impact for the minimum of fuss. Some involve special construction or sewing techniques, and these are accompanied by detailed step-by-step illustrations and instructions. Many, however, are just simple, ingenious ideas that you can execute almost instantly.

The following chapters are organized according to room – living room, bedroom, and so on – but most of the projects are easy to adapt for use anywhere in your home. Imagine the flanged cushion from the kitchen chapter on a huge squashy sofa, or picture the reefed curtains in a formal living room or study instead of the nursery. Discover for yourself the feel and the look of crisp cotton and linen, rich slubby silk, soft wool, luxurious fringe, and heavy, hanging tassels. Once you start experimenting, you may feel inspired, confident, and ambitious enough to begin inventing your own unique and original ways to bring your rooms irresistibly to life with textiles and trimmings.

The colour of these lavish yet simple curtains brings a touch of opulence to an otherwise plain and dark room. The curtains also cleverly highlight the jewel-like triangles in the antique patchwork table cover. In addition, hints of the same shade appear on the cushion covers adorning the plain window seat, thereby helping to unify the two sections of the room.

CHAPTER TWO

Living Rooms

During the early Middle Ages, all family activities including cooking and sleeping were carried on in a single chamber: the Great Hall. Not since then, however, has as much been demanded of a single domestic space as modern households ask of their – very much smaller – living rooms. To begin with, most of us look to this room to provide a nurturing environment at the end of the day – one in which we can read, watch television, listen to music, play games, or just talk to family and friends. At the same time, we often want it to act as a home office or even as somewhere we can pursue our hobbies. Then, with the very minimum of extra effort, we expect the same room to be on semi-permanent public show: a gracious and elegant venue for entertaining, and an expression of our own tastes and interests.

In order for your living room to fulfil all these expectations, it has to be comfortable, thoroughly practical, and decorative, and your choice of soft furnishings and textiles can contribute a great deal towards bringing this about. To begin with, always invest in top-quality seating as no one will be able to relax on uncomfortable chairs and sofas. What's more, they are often the focal point of the room. Make sure any fabric you choose for upholstery is suitable for its purpose, both in weight and in colour. Good shops will tell you if

To create a room that looks sophisticated and dramatic yet cosy at the same time, combine deep colours and different patterns with a wealth of stylish accessories; cover chairs, sofas, and tables with contrasting shawls and blankets; make contrasting tartan armcaps and stack the sofa full of cushions with various textures, in colours that blend with the scheme.

At the opposite end of our living room, an exotic, ethnic atmosphere has been evoked with a selection of Oriental textiles: a fringed carpet, an antique patchwork wallhanging, and a paisley shawl as a tablecloth. This unlikely partnership of baronial, Elizabethan, and Indian furnishings works well because all of the items have a similar intensity of colour.

a material is intended only for curtains, but you'll have to make your own colour choices. If your household consists of careful adults who use the living room only for formal occasions, pale hues could work well. Where there are young children and animals, however, deeper shades are a much wiser choice. Try to select a scheme that can adapt to a wide range of people and activities over a long period of time.

For our living room, we've chosen a rich, traditional palette based around burgundy, dark green, and cream. With it, we've combined graceful period furniture plus an eclectic mix of accessories including antique needlework cushions, modern lampshades, and exotic textiles that infuse the room with luxury and opulence. Interpreted differently, however, the same elements could produce a variety of looks. To create a warm country atmosphere choose softer, lighter colours and replace the sophisticated pattern of the curtains with a plain shade, a simple stripe, or a rustic floral print. Instead of ethnic throws, drape pretty quilts over the sofas, chairs, or tables, and hang an embroidered sampler or a beautiful quilt on the wall. Make a pile of assorted cushions in wool or cotton rather than velvet and tapestry, and cover the floor with hooked or braided rugs laid over coir matting.

FRINGED PELMET

For the living room window we wanted a plain pelmet (cornice) that would smarten the room and add a touch of formality, but we were somewhat restricted by the space available. Our solution was to choose a pattern of broad stripes for our curtains, and simply cut out one of the stripes plus a border on both sides of it to use as a pelmet. Stiffened with buckram or interfacing, and mounted on a wooden board with Velcro, the fabric strip was finished off with a length of grosgrain braid at the top, and a fringe along the lower edge in coordinating shades.

A popular variation of this straight pelmet is a shaped version in which the hem has been cut into scallops, points, or castellations, using a paper template centred across the pelmet.

YOU WILL NEED

STRIP OF MAIN CURTAIN FABRIC

MATCHING SEWING THREAD

CURTAIN LINING FABRIC FOR THE BACK OF
THE PELMET

INTERFACING OR BUCKRAM, AS DEEP AS
PELMET

STRIP OF BRAID FOR THE TOP EDGE

FRINGED BRAID FOR THE LOWER EDGE

ALL-PURPOSE GLUE, SUITABLE FOR FABRIC

VELCRO (WITH BOTH STRIPS SELF-ADHESIVE)

PELMET (CORNICE) BOARD OR 2.5CM (1IN)
BATTEN HELD BY ANGLE IRONS

MEASURING

Measure along the length of the pelmet (cornice) board or batten, including the sides, and cut the main fabric and lining to this measurement plus 2.5cm (1in) and to the desired finished depth plus 2.5cm (1in).

Cut interfacing to the required finished size, without seam allowances.

1 Lay the main fabric piece face down on a flat surface, and place the interfacing on top, with an even 12mm (½in) of main fabric showing all around each edge.

2 Lockstitch the interfacing to the fabric with vertical lines of lock-stitching, starting at the centre and working outwards at approximately 20cm (8in) intervals. To lockstitch, fold the interfacing back on itself and secure the thread to the back of it at the top. Take a stitch through the interfacing and the fabric close to the fold, picking up only a couple of threads of each. Pass the needle through the loop of thread and make another stitch about 5cm (2in) further along the fold. Continue in the same way, lockstitching down the fold, then fasten off the thread.

3 Fold the 12mm (½in) turning allowance on each edge of the main fabric over to the back, trimming across the allowance at corners and making mitred folds.

4 Secure the turnings to the interfacing at the back using herringbone stitch (blind catchstitch). Work this from left to right with the needle pointing left, taking small stitches in the fabric and the edge of the turning alternately.

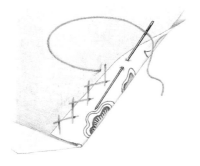

5 Turn under and press a 1.5cm (⅝in) turning on each side of the lining fabric, mitring the corners, as for the main fabric. Slipstitch the lining to the back of the main fabric around all four sides, making sure that the lining cannot be seen from the front of the pelmet. Work slipstitch from right to left, picking up just a few threads of the lining fabric, then passing the needle inside the folded edge of the

A length of plain braid and fan edging in mixed shades of red, green, and cream provide the perfect decorative finish for our pelmet (cornice) board.

lining for about 6mm (¼in). Bring the needle out and pick up a few threads of the main fabric exactly opposite the point it came out. Insert the needle into the fold opposite this point and continue in the same way.

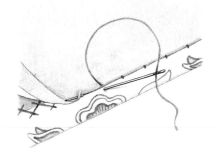

6 On the right side of the pelmet, glue the straight-edged braid strip along the top edge. Glue the fringed braid along the lower edge of the pelmet.

7 Stick the looped strip of Velcro to the back of the pelmet, running about 6mm (¼in) below the top edge. Stick the corresponding hooked strip along the pelmet board or batten. Press the finished pelmet into place.

OTTOMAN

Remarkably functional as well as decorative, the ottoman first became popular in the early nineteenth century, its design derived from the upholstered benches covered with cushions used in the Ottoman Empire. By the Victorian era it was being used in every room of the house, in both circular and rectangular forms and a variety of fabrics. The box ottoman, with its padded, hinged lid, was a particularly versatile piece of Victorian furniture still popular today.

Essentially a large, padded box covered in fabric, the box ottoman is fairly easy to make using a plain wooden blanket box or a metal trunk as a base. The finished product will not only have a softer, warmer look than a coffee table, but its height will also make it more convenient to use. As a bonus, it has lots of useful storage space inside, and it can even serve as an extra seat when necessary.

We've covered our box ottoman with a corner-pleated loose cover made from furnishing cotton printed in a subtle red-and-green check. Alternatively, for a rich Victorian look, cover your box closely with a thick fabric; a tapestry weave, sound portions of an old kelim or oriental rug, or even a worn quilt, would be ideal, and any leftover bits would make stunning cushion covers. An embroidered Indian fabric or a soft pile material such as chenille would also work well. Finally, cover the raw edges on the inside with gimp (a type of braid designed to fit smoothly around curves) or other braid.

YOU WILL NEED

PLAIN CHEST OR BLANKET BOX WITHOUT
COMPLICATED REBATE ON THE LID
SOFT FURNISHING FABRIC
MATCHING SEWING THREAD
FOAM CUSHIONING, 4CM (1½IN) THICK
ALL-PURPOSE GLUE
STAPLE GUN, OR HAMMER AND SMALL NAILS
BRAID SUCH AS GIMP

MEASURING

For the lid, cut a piece of fabric to the dimensions of the top of the lid plus 15cm (6in) on each dimension. For the skirt, cut a piece of fabric to the height of the base plus 7.5cm (3in) by the perimeter plus 82.5cm (33in).

1 Remove the hinges from the chest while you are making and fitting the fabric covering.

2 Cut the foam to the correct size for the top of the chest, bevelling the top edges slightly. A well-sharpened carving knife is easier to use than scissors for this. Glue the foam to the lid of the chest.

3 Stretch the lid fabric firmly over the foam, folding it neatly at the corners and stapling or nailing it in place on the underside of the lid. Staple from the centres of two opposite sides out to the edges, and then staple the other two sides in the same way.

4 At the rebates for the hinges, use a craft knife to trim away the fabric. Glue the fabric down around the cut edges. If the fabric is not too bulky and the rebates are sufficiently deep, you may be able simply to screw the hinges back over the fabric.

5 When you have finished covering the lid top, glue gimp or other braid over the raw edge of the fabric.

6 With right sides together and taking a 12mm (½in) seam allowance, join the two short sides of the skirt, making it into a loop. Press the seam open. Along the lower edge, make a double 12mm (½in) hem; slipstitch.

7 With the fabric wrong side out, and the seam at centre back, measure and mark on the skirt where the corners of the box will be, allowing 20cm (8in) extra fabric at each corner for the pleat. Fold the extra fabric in half and pin to form a 10cm (4in) pleat at each corner. Put the skirt over the box and adjust as necessary to make it fit. For each pleat, stitch 10cm (4in) from the fold, along the pinned line, in a vertical line running down for 11.5cm (4½in) from the top, raw edge.

8 Turn the fabric right side out and form the pleats into inverted pleats, by flattening each with the seam running down the middle. Baste each pleat along the top, raw edge, and press the whole length of each pleat.

9 Place the skirt over the chest, bringing the hem evenly down to floor level. Fold the raw edge over to the inside of the box and staple or nail it in position. If the pleats are too bulky, you may need to cut away the folded fabric from the back of the pleat – but do this only from the point where it folds over the edge of the box and then hold the pleats in place by gluing the fabric to the top of the chest.

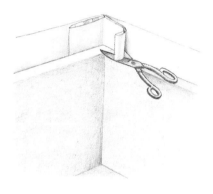

10 Cover the raw edge on the inside of the chest with braid, as for the lid.

11 To finish the ottoman, replace the hinges. You may need to remove fabric at the hinge rebates, as for the lid.

Our ottoman has a corner-pleated loose cover made from crisp upholstery cotton. For a completely different look, pad your box on all five exposed sides and give it a close-fitted cover of heavy tapestry-weave fabric, embroidered crewelwork, thick, soft chenille, or even sound portions of a worn kelim, an Oriental pile rug, or an old quilt. To conceal the raw edges and joins, tack or glue on lengths of thick cord or braid.

To customize a plain, ready-made lampshade instantly, attach a length of coordinating braid, fringe, or ribbon at the bottom, or tie a big, bold tassel around the top.

PLEATED LAMPSHADE

Instead of seeing lampshades as plain and utilitarian adjuncts to a carefully chosen base, look on them as stylish accessories in their own right – accessories that can pick up the colours used elsewhere in your room, or provide a bright, unexpected accent in a neutral scheme. There's no need to restrict yourself to ready-made shades, when you can use fabric to create designs that suit your taste and your rooms. If you've never made a lampshade before, you will probably find a gathered shade easier than a flat one.

Whatever your choice, the starting point is a wire frame. These are available in a range of basic shapes, from straight cylinders (or drums) to waisted cylinders (bowed drums) and those that increase in size from top to bottom (tapered drums). New frames are available fairly widely, or look for an old, torn shade with a pretty or unusual shape. If the frame is still sound, it can be re-used, but be sure to strip off all the old fabric and tape, then remove any traces of rust. You could add a coat of paint or varnish at this stage to discourage further rusting.

When it comes to choosing a covering fabric, be guided initially by the function your lamp has to fulfil – if you want it mainly to provide an atmospheric pool of illumination in a dark corner, you can use any light- or medium-weight material in any colour you fancy. If your lamp is intended for a work or reading area, however, choose a thinnish material (such as silk or cotton) in a pale colour – dress fabrics are ideal. Finish off the edges with a length of self-piping, narrow braid, or cord.

Making an ordinary flat lampshade normally involves preparing the frame for covering by binding it with cotton tape to which the cover can eventually be stitched. Also, most shades should be lined to make the struts less obvious when the lamp is lit: flame-retardant silk is the best choice for this purpose, but fine cotton is often used instead. White will let through the most light. The pleated construction of our shade, however, successfully disguises the struts, so lining isn't necessary. We've simplified the process even further by using glue to attach the cover instead of sewing it in place.

YOU WILL NEED

COOLIE LAMPSHADE FRAME
FABRIC
MATCHING SEWING THREAD
LONG PINS
MASKING TAPE
ALL-PURPOSE GLUE, SUITABLE FOR FABRIC

1 Measure around the base of your lampshade and around the top rim. You will require a strip of bias binding for each. Cut 5cm (2in) wide binding strips from the fabric (or from a contrast fabric), allowing 1.5cm (⅝in) extra for the join on each.

2 Measure the (sloping) length from top to base of the coolie shade. Cutting on the crosswise grain, cut a rectangle of fabric to this measurement plus an allowance of 2.5cm (1in). The length of the rectangle should be about 1½ times the circumference of the lower rim, to allow for the pleats, plus a further 2.5cm (1in).

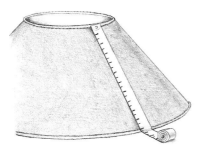

3 With right sides together, join the short edges, taking a 12mm (½in) seam allowance. Neaten the edges and press the seam open. Divide the fabric into

quarters, marking it with small notches at the top and bottom. Divide the shade into quarters to correspond, lightly marking it at top and bottom.

4 Slip the fabric over the shade and form the pleats. Use small strips of masking tape projecting from behind the rim at the top and bottom of the shade to hold the fabric steady as you pleat. (Having pre-cut strips of masking tape ready beforehand will make this easier.) Pin each pleat at the top and bottom as you form it.

5 When you are happy with the arrangement, trim away the excess fabric from around the top and bottom, then remove the fabric from the shade. Baste around the top and bottom edges to hold the pleats, and remove the pins.

Even if your lamp is intended to provide atmospheric rather than working illumination, because of the pleating or gathering the fabric you choose for its shade should be fairly lightweight and not bulky.

6 Press the long raw edges of the bias binding strips inwards to meet down the centre (see page 57, step 5). Pin and baste one strip to cover the raw edges at the bottom of the shade and one at the top.

7 Where the ends of the bias binding meet, turn back one end for 6mm (¼in) and overlap the other end for about 9mm (⅜in). Topstitch the bias binding in place, stitching close to the folded edges.

8 Place the finished fabric cover over the shade, using a few touches of glue around the rims to hold it in place.

SMOCKED CUSHION

Smocking was first developed as a decorative way of gathering the fabric of a garment into regular folds. Its best-known application was on the traditional loose shirt worn by English country workmen from early Saxon times onwards; known as a smock (the Anglo-Saxon word for shift or chemise) this shirt gave its name to the technique used to shape and decorate it. Over time, this decoration became increasingly elaborate, until by the early nineteenth century, each shirt was adorned with intricate patterns that reflected its owner's occupation: trees and leaves for a woodman; wheels for a wheel-maker, or carter; and crooks for a shepherd.

Today, smocking is used mainly on special items of clothing for babies and children, but in a larger, simplified version it can also give a rich, textural, and delightfully unusual finish to ordinary throw cushions. For our example, we've chosen a fabric with a large check, which not only suits the rather graphic effect of jumbo smocking very well, but also provides a built-in guide for the stitches. (The check must be woven in rather than printed because prints do not always follow the lengthwise and crosswise grain exactly, and these must be followed when smocking.) On a plain colour, the pattern would stand out even more clearly (though without the checks you'd have to draw out guidelines on the back). Small, discreet prints can also look very pretty embellished with smocking, but complex, multi-coloured patterns can sometimes over-shadow the stitching.

Slightly easier ideas include inserting a smocked panel across the centre of a cushion cover or smocking only the flanged border, stitching it on after smocking.

YOU WILL NEED

WOVEN CHECKED FABRIC
MATCHING SEWING THREAD
STRANDED EMBROIDERY THREAD (FLOSS)
ZIP
CUSHION PAD

1 The smocking is done first. The gathers will reduce the overall size of the fabric piece, and the scale of the smocking will largely depend on the nature of your fabric, so make an experimental piece first to work out the unsmocked and smocked dimen-sions. Note that the size increases slightly when the gathering threads are removed after smocking (step 6). Allow extra fabric all around for a 4cm (1½in) flat edge and a 12mm (½in) seam allowance.

2 Using sewing thread, work lines of running stitch across the fabric square in one direction, following the bands of colour. With each of these gathering threads, start with a knot and insert the needle only at the corners of the squares. Align the stitches in each row, so that when the fabric is gathered, folds of one colour will be brought to the front. At the end of each row, leave a few centimetres (an inch or so) of loose thread. Unlike the other ends, these should not be knotted.

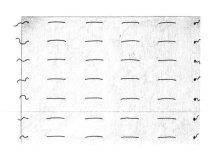

3 When you have made enough rows of gathering threads for the desired size of your cushion, hold all the thread ends together and gently push the fabric along the threads, forming regular folds. Gently pull the fabric lengthwise as you ease it along.

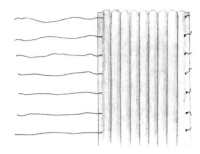

4 When you have finished, ease the fabric out until it is slightly less than the required finished width and you can see the gathering threads between pleats. The cushion cover in the picture has been very loosely smocked – just enough to draw elements of the check design together in an open pattern – so to achieve a similar effect you will not need to have the gathering threads drawn tightly. Tie the un-knotted ends in pairs, to hold them while you smock.

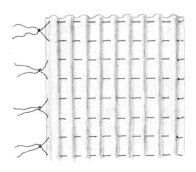

5 The smocking stitch used here is honeycomb stitch. Thread your needle with stranded embroidery cotton (floss). Use two strands, if they will pass easily through the fabric, otherwise use just one strand. Bring your needle out on the left of the first pleat at the top left-hand corner of the gathering. Take it over the second pleat and through to the left side of the first pleat, bringing it out immediately below the first exit point. Make a second stitch just below the first – you should now have one stitch just above the gathering line and a second just below it. This time take the needle down behind the fabric to the gathering line just below and bring it out on the left side of the second pleat; make two stitches over the second and third pleats. Now go back up to the first row and make two stitches over the third and fourth pleats. Continue in this way, smocking pairs of rows, until you have smocked the whole gathered area.

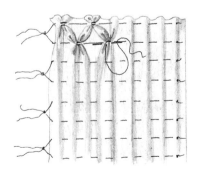

6 Remove the gathering threads, and gently stretch the smocked fabric out to the required width. Stitch the folds flat along the outer, unsmocked edge of the fabric.

The woven-in checks of the fabric provide stitching guidelines when smocking.

7 For the back of the cushion, cut two pieces of fabric, each the desired finished width of the cushion plus 2.5cm (1in) for seam allowances, and half the desired finished depth plus 4cm (1½in). Taking a 2.5cm (1in) seam allowance, stitch the two pieces together, leaving a gap in the centre for a zip. Insert the zip into the seam.

8 With the zip open, lay the back piece on the front piece with right sides together, and stitch all the way around the outer edge, taking a 12mm (½in) seam allowance.

9 Turn the fabric right side out, close the zip, and stitch again along the inner edge of the border, next to the smocking. Open the zip and insert the cushion pad into the smocked cover.

DECORATING EXISTING CUSHIONS

Even when you don't make your cushion covers from scratch, there are lots of ways you can stamp your personality on ready-made ones.

One way is to find some interesting trimming. A simple idea is to sew a length of fat cord, matching or contrasting, around the outside. Alternatively, attach large tassels to each corner for a dramatic look, or scatter multi-coloured small tassels over the surface. You could sew mattress-style tufts on the surface, or, alternatively, stitch straight or curved fringe around the edges of a cover. Wide silk, velvet, or grosgrain ribbon looks pretty layered in slightly overlapping rows, or use braid, curvy gimp, or a

tasselled fringe perhaps in a design woven with gold for a more opulent look. Another idea is to hand sew dainty old lace doilies or hand-kerchiefs onto small cushions, and tray cloths or antimacassars onto larger ones.

To give old cushions a completely new look, make covers that simply tie on, involving only the most rudimentary needlework. You can do this in two ways. The first is by cutting two pieces of fabric slightly larger than your pad, hemming both of them, then tying them together with strips of fabric stitched to each corner and halfway along each side – or use lengths of cord or ribbon. If you're a little more ambitious, you could cut your squares slightly larger, and sew buttonholes along the edges of one and buttons on the other. The second type of tie-on cover is most suitable for square cushions. To make it, cut a square of fabric with sides twice as long as those of your cushion (plus hem allowance). Hem it, then attach ties to each corner. Lay this square flat, hems uppermost, and place your cushion on top so that each corner points to the mid-point of one of the square's sides. Now fold over the corners and tie them together, envelope style.

Linked by rich colours and textures, these decorative cushions have all been trimmed to suit their original style: multi-colour tasselled clusters on plain velvet, simple braid bordering intricate tapestrywork, tasselled fringe around a tapestry picture, and rows of tiny cowrie shells setting off an exotically geometric design worked in appliqué.

TABLECLOTHS

Tablecloths are often regarded only as washable protective coverings brought out at mealtimes, but tables of every description offer an ideal display surface for a wide variety of beautiful textiles. Soft folds of fabric will, of course, do far more to give rooms a rich, comfortable look than hard, shiny surfaces, and they also provide a stylish disguise for tables that have become scuffed or stained over the years.

Rugs or small carpets can be beautiful table coverings. The idea has a solid historical base – when Oriental carpets were first imported in the Middle Ages, they were usually draped on tables, being far too precious to go on the floor. In fact, the term table carpet referred for some time to any fabric that fulfilled this function – small floor coverings were called foot carpets. The practice was still widespread in the sixteenth century. Today, in Belgium and Holland, soft-pile Oriental-looking table carpets are still manufactured, and in common use. You can achieve a similar look with an old or modern flat-pile rug such as a kelim or a dhurry; the secret is to choose one soft and thin enough to hang gracefully.

Another way to get the same thick, textural feeling is with a woollen blanket, perhaps woven with a simple check, or an old quilt – plain, printed, or patchwork. For small tables, look for an embroidered silk shawl, or one made from light wool like the paisley design we've chosen. To turn an ordinary table into a pretty dressing table, simply drape it with a length of soft muslin or colourful chintz. Protective sheets of glass cut to size with bevelled edges, make a good covering for a fragile or antique textile.

THROW-OVER COVERS FOR SOFAS AND CHAIRS

Whether your decorating style is traditional, exotic, or streamlined and modern, use informal throw-over covers to give your sofas and chairs a dramatic new look instantly. Large pieces of fabric that have some thickness and weight are the most suitable; a quilt is ideal, as is a blanket, a bedspread, an old-fashioned chenille tablecloth, or a length of suitable fabric. A quilt or a checked blanket would give a country look, while a length of heavy linen or cotton duck (canvas or sailcloth) or a plain woollen bed-spread, would be right for a more minimalist scheme. A large paisley throw or a soft rug would add grandeur to any room. Consider changing the covers with the seasons, choosing dark, cosy ones for winter, and fresh, bright ones for the sunny days of summer.

Make sure that the textiles you choose are more than large enough to cover your chairs or sofas completely, so that any movement in the cover won't leave large expanses of seat or arm exposed. Some degree of anchoring is possible with corner ties, but don't attempt to pin or stitch the material in position, since any tension could cause it to tear. The casual, slightly rumpled look of a draped cover is an integral part of its charm.

If you don't want to adopt this idea wholesale, adapt it slightly by giving your upholstered seating conventional loose or fitted covers in plain, neutral colours, then adding more richly coloured layered throws on top in the form of small blankets or quilts, tartan picnic rugs, silk or woollen shawls, or large scarves.

TIE-BACKS

Curtain tie-backs are both practical and decorative. By holding curtains back, they admit the maximum amount of light and at the same time create a graceful shape. A variety of effects is possible, depending on where the tie-backs are positioned. In many cases, they are also beautiful in their own right. Traditional tie-backs are made from thick cord, with or without tassels, but you can create an almost infinite number of designs by improvising your own.

In choosing the materials for our tie-backs, we turned to the traditional country saddler's workshop, where we found leather straps, brass hardware, and rope girths that could be combined in lots of ways. Ethnic saddlery is another rich source of inspiration; in India and Arabia, camels and horses are adorned with beautiful woven tapestries and textiles, which you could be lucky enough to find in antique shops or markets.

For an exotic touch, fasten your drapes with ethnic beads or bells collected on holiday or unearthed in specialist shops. Sew hooks on the ends of Indian embroidery or mirrorwork strips to turn them into tie-backs. Knot lovely silk scarves around wall-fixed rings. Plait chunky tie-backs from three double skeins of thick tapestry wool or yarn. Delicate curtains would look enchanting fastened with strips of lace border or silk or embroidered ribbon.

Elaborate, multi-coloured tie-backs look best on plain curtains, since their effect would be swamped by a busy print. When you've decided on the construction, experiment with various effects. Move the tie-backs up and down to create different shapes in the curtains, or adjust the amount of fabric that drapes over the tie-backs to give anything from a soft, billowing effect to a taut, tailored look.

TOP LEFT This chunky tie-back was made to order from a country saddler, but you could achieve a similar look by using a heavy leather belt, either plain or plaited.

TOP RIGHT Anchor your curtains with strands of ethnic beads. If there is not too much fullness, they might be long enough on their own; otherwise, tie them onto lengths of rope or raffia.

BOTTOM LEFT Strips of Indian needlework make unique and colourful tie-backs; this one is adorned with tiny chips of mirror, but other typical examples feature embroidery, cutwork, or appliqué.

BOTTOM RIGHT Here, the curtain was caught back with a piece of antique Turkish saddlery – a tasselled girth strap woven in a flamestitch pattern, the colours of which echo those of the floral print.

In this quintessentially Victorian scheme, the fireplace mantel has been given a fitted chintz skirt that is characteristic of the period and matches the room's curtains exactly, right down to its matching trim of three-coloured tasselled fringe.

Another shaped pelmet (cornice), this time cut in a castellated, or stepped, design. A contrasting braid border emphasizes its strong, graphic lines and matches the one on the full-length curtains. To avoid a fussy look, the tie-backs have been kept simple.

OPPOSITE Combine geometrics and florals imaginatively. Here, a loose, painterly floral has been used symmetrically with a ticking stripe to upholster the sofa in a patchwork effect. The cushions add to the mix-and-match look with a smaller-scale coordinated floral, the same yellow stripes and green stripes but with the addition of another, simpler stripe too.

ABOVE When a window sits in an
awkward recess, a single curtain is often
the best solution. Draw up the gathered
or pleated heading until it fits the angle
exactly, then fix the curtain
permanently in position. During the day,
hold it to one side with a traditional
tie-back or a large brass arm hold-back.

RIGHT In this stylish Manhattan interior,
long full curtains in slubby neutral fabric
have been topped with a fabric-covered
wooden pelmet (cornice), shaped into
dramatic harlequin points and edged
with a wide beige and white stripe.

CHAPTER THREE

Dining Rooms

The place where family and friends get together to share food, wine, and conversation has a central part to play in the social life of any household, whether meals are taken in a separate room, or a corner of the living room or kitchen. This has been true since the end of the seventeenth century. By then it had become increasingly common for aristocratic families to dine not in the vast dining hall where they had previously taken their meals with servants and retainers, but in a smaller, more private anteroom. A much more pleasant and practical space than its predecessor, this chamber contained a circular or oval table that servants could get around easily, a set of chairs, and a sideboard ("cup-board") which was used for storage and serving. Since that time, the dining room's function and furnishing have changed very little. With a bit of thought and effort, however, you can give your mealtime surroundings the extra touch of style and comfort that encourages contemporary diners to linger chatting long after the plates have been cleared away.

This dining room owes its refreshing quality to the white linen curtains, and white painted walls, and cream chairs accessorised with fresh greens and blues. The balance of contemporary and period characteristics is what gives it such a homely but modern feeling. The antique gilt overmantel reflects the airy view, while the malachite green commode brings the colour of the outdoors inside. The natural coir carpeting, large-scale floral chair skirts, use of coloured glass rather than silver, and checked tablecloth add informality to an otherwise formal room.

A separate dining room offers a unique design opportunity; as long as the space can adapt in appearance and operation to a range of meals from hurried breakfasts and casual lunches to special events such as Christmas dinner, you can experiment with almost any colour scheme or decorative style. Because comparatively short periods of time are spent here, bold hues and dramatic effects that might be overpowering in a living room or kitchen often work extremely well. In terms of textiles and soft furnishings, there is enormous scope to explore the potential not only of conventional elements such as curtains and loose covers, but also of the table itself. Your choice of table linen – cloths, place-mats, napkins and trimmings – can completely alter both the look of the room and the atmosphere of the occasion.

In our spacious dining room we've used a scheme inspired by Swedish country interiors: pale colours and a mixture of formal, restrained furniture and crisp, bright fabrics. Cool white walls, natural coir matting, and simple arrangements of fruit and flowers on the table and sideboard help to create a pastoral look, while huge French windows allow the greenery outside to become, even in winter, an important part of the room's rustic charm.

Using exactly the same elements, you could just as easily create the warm, opulent look associated with houses of the Victorian period. If this effect appeals, choose richly patterned wallpaper instead of painted walls, and hang curtains of crimson or deep forest green. In place of fabric borders, trim the self-pelmet (integral valance) with heavy plain or tasselled fringe. On the dining chairs, replace the box-pleated loose covers with fitted ones edged in braid or bullion fringe. As a final touch, lay the table with a cloth of snowy damask, and matching napkins caught up in velvet ribbon.

SELF-PELMET CURTAINS

When your curtains hang from a lovely wooden or brass pole, a simple, graceful self-pelmet (integral valance) can be extremely appealing. It flatters all types of windows, from small, deep ones in an old stone cottage to tall, bow-fronted ones in a Victorian townhouse. And because the self-pelmet pulls back along with the curtains when they are opened, it lets in more light than a fixed pelmet (cornice or valance).

Traditionally a pelmet should be about one-fifth to one-quarter of the length of the curtains, but there is no need to stick to this rule slavishly. You can make a self-pelmet in various ways. One simple method is to cut and stitch a separate piece, like a mini-curtain, then slip it into the same rings as the main fabric panels. The self-pelmet can either match the main fabric, coordinate with it subtly, or contrast completely. A second, and even easier, way of achieving this look is possible only with materials that are identical on both sides, such as most woven and plain fabrics, tartans, and flannels. It involves simply attaching your heading tape a little way down from the top of each fabric drop so that the excess flops over in front. Turn the raw edges under, or finish them with a length of fringe or a border.

One very pretty version of this simple idea is to make an almost no-sew sheer curtain from a cotton or linen lace tablecloth or bedspread, which will create enchanting patterns of dappled light on a sunny day. Measure your window and find a piece of cloth longer than the height of the window and roughly 1½ times the width. The edges and hems will be finished already, so all you have to do is sew on the heading tape. The depth of your heading will, of course, vary, but a heading of less than about 15cm (6 in) may look too scanty. (For an even easier self-pelmet curtain that involves no sewing at all, see the illustration on page 86.)

The self-pelmet curtains in our dining room are lined and have handmade pinch pleats. This technique is only suitable for a very lightweight fabric such as silk, or this openweave linen, as step 8 requires sewing through a number of thicknesses. The self-pelmet is edged in a contrast fabric also used for the tablecloth.

YOU WILL NEED

MAIN CURTAIN FABRIC

LINING FABRIC

CONTRAST FABRIC

MATCHING SEWING THREAD

BUCKRAM

MEASURING

First measure the width of the curtain track or pole and the length of the drop (allow extra if, as here, the curtain is to be longer than floor length so it pools onto the floor).

Main fabric

For generous pleats of this type, you will need three times the width of the finished pleated curtains to be safe. Choose a fabric that can be used in full widths to make up the total width required, adjusting the spacing between the pleats and the amount of fabric necessary for the pleats to accommodate a slightly greater or lesser total width. (If your window requires three widths of fabric for two curtains, sew the three widths together and cut down the middle of the complete width so the pattern matches in the middle when the curtains are drawn.) Calculate the fabric requirement of each curtain individually before adding up the total fabric requirements for all the curtains.

Width

As an example, the triple pleats shown here were spaced 15cm (6in) apart, and each pleat used up 18cm (7in) of fabric, a fairly standard arrangement for this size of curtain. This means that to cover 45cm (17in) of track, you will require 81cm (32 in) of fabric (two pleats and three spaces) plus allow 4cm (1½ in) for each side hem and 2.5cm (1in) (or one pattern repeat) for seams where fabric widths must be joined. You will need to make your own calculations for your window. It is a good idea to sketch your calculations on paper as we have.

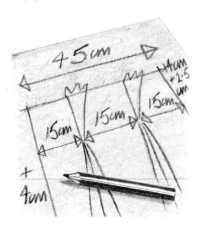

Measurement of the triple pleat may also depend on your pattern, especially if you have a stripe in which case the pattern should guide your calculations.

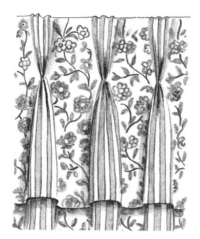

For each width of curtain (and lining) fabric, allow a full drop, plus 2.5cm (1 in) at the top and at least 10cm (4in) at the bottom for hems. To be safe, you can allow an extra 20cm (8in) for hems at the top and bottom in case of crooked floors or walls.

Self-pelmet

You will also require fabric for the self-pelmet (integral valance). To suit the long window here, this was made 40cm (16in) deep: allow a depth on the main fabric of 40cm (16in) – no hem allowance is added, as this is provided by the contrast band. Multiply this by the number of widths required for the curtain in order to find the total length of main fabric required for the pelmet. Add this to the fabric needed for the main curtain.

Lining

For each curtain, you will require enough fabric to make up the width of the finished curtain, including pleats, but without any extra side turning allowance. Allow 10cm (4in) for the top and bottom hem. For the pelmet, you will require the same amount of lining fabric as main fabric, but without side turning allowances.

Contrast band

Allow the same number of fabric widths as for the main fabric (assuming both are the same width). Our contrast band was to be 5cm (2in) finished depth (it also had a fabric repeat of 5cm or 2in). To calculate the depth of fabric, allow 5cm (2in) for finished depth plus 5cm (2in) for back of contrast band, plus 2 x 2.5cm (1in) hem – a total of 15cm (6in). As an example, if each curtain will use two widths of fabric, and you are making two curtains altogether, you will require 2 x 2 x 15cm (6 in) = 60cm (24in) of contrast fabric.

Buckram

For each curtain, you will require a 10cm (4in) deep band of buckram to the width of the finished curtain.

MAKING THE CURTAINS

1 Cut the main and lining fabric into the correct number of drops for all the curtains and pelmets. For each curtain, start by joining widths of main fabric and of lining fabric. Do the same for the pelmet lengths, and set these aside.

2 *Main curtain:* Press 4cm (1½in) to the side edges and 10cm (4in) at the bottom hem, mitre the corners, and slipstitch (see page 17) the hem.

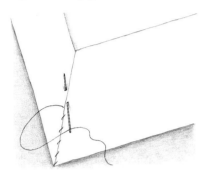

Lining the main curtain: Cut the lining widths a total of 5cm (2in) less than the main curtain fabric finished width. Fold and press a double 5cm (2in) hem at the bottom and machine stitch. Then fold 2.5cm (1in) hem at the side edges and slipstitch the lining 5cm (2in) above the bottom of the main curtain fabric, wrong sides together. Measure the finished height plus 2.5cm (1in) seam allowance and cut off any excess fabric and lining at the top edge of the curtain.

3 *Pelmet:* Measure and cut the main fabric and lining width the same as the curtain width before pleating, leaving side seams open for the moment (do not join main fabric and lining yet). Join strips of contrast fabric to make the full length, then fold the strip, with wrong sides together, and press down the centre. Unfold, and join the contrast strip to the bottom edge of the pelmet, with right sides together and taking a 2.5cm (1in) seam. Press the seam open then press 4cm (1½in)

turnings at the side edges of the main fabric and border. Take the contrast strip to the wrong side, along the folded edge, mitring the corners. Turn the raw edges under for a depth of 2.5cm (1in) and press.

Lining the pelmet: Fold 2.5cm (1in) at the sides edges and hem of the lining. Place the lining and main pelmet fabric wrong sides together bringing the pressed edge of the contrast band over the lower edge of the lining. Slipstitch the lining to the main fabric at the sides and along the edge of the contrast band. Measure the finished height of the pelmet plus a 2.5cm (1in) hem allowance at the top and trim off all the excess fabric along the top raw edge.

4 *Joining main curtain and pelmet:* Place the right side of the top raw edge of the pelmet to the wrong side of the raw edge of the curtain and machine stitch a 2.5cm (1in) seam.

5 Press the seam open. Fold the pelmet over to the right side of the curtain along the stitched line and place the buckram in between the curtain and pelmet with the edge along the seamline. Press buckram in place.

6 Slipstitch the side edges of the curtain to the pelmet from the top edge down to the bottom of the buckram so the buckram does not show at the sides.

7 *Pleats:* Mark the position of the pleats along the back of the curtain. Use dressmaker's chalk or marking pencil and draw vertical lines down from the top edge, spacing the lines so that there is the correct space between each pleat, and the correct allowance that you have calculated for each pleat.

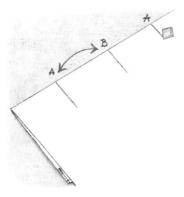

A self-pelmet (integral valance) makes a refreshing and practical change from a traditional, separate pelmet. Here, the skilled mix of formal and country-fresh that epitomizes the Swedish country look is represented by prim pinch-pleats and an unpretentious checked cotton border.

8 For each pleat, bring together the marked pleat lines (A & B in previous illustration) and stitch down from the top of the curtain to a depth of 10cm (4in). If your machine cannot cope with so many thicknesses of fabric, you may have to stitch these folds by hand. Fold each pleat into a triple fold by hand, and then stitch from the bottom of the stitched pleat line to the edge of the folds by hand, stitching through all thicknesses.

9 Insert pin hooks into lining and buckram at back of curtain, at the base of each pleat.

ZIG-ZAG TABLECLOTH

Although ready-made tablecloths are sold in a wide range of colours and patterns, you can expand the available selection almost endlessly by sewing one yourself. Not only does this enable you to choose from a huge range of fabrics, but it also means you can have a cloth in any size you want. (To make an extra-wide one without any seams, use cotton sheeting.) You can also add your own choice of details or trimmings. One unusual touch is a novelty border; we've made a zig-zag edge, but your tablecloth could have gentle scallops, or a stepped, castellated shape.

Our tablecloth was very easily made from two joined pieces of fabric – the same as that used for the contrast binding on the curtains – and the edges were simply cut with pinking shears. These should not fray too much, but as a precaution they could be sprayed with roller blind (roller shade) stiffener. If the tablecloth is likely to be used a lot and require frequent washing, it would be preferable to machine satin-stitch the edges, as described here.

A set of matching napkins could be given the same treatment, with the scale of the cut-out design reduced in proportion to their size. You could even echo the geometric theme elsewhere in the room, adding your chosen shape to the edges of curtains, pelmets (cornices), loose covers, cushions, or lampshades.

Another easy way to add interest to table linen is by sewing on a fabric border or a length of suitable trimming such as ribbon, wide cotton lace, or pompon fringe – again, decorate the napkins to match for a coordinated look. Make sure that any trimming you choose is not only machine-washable, but also pre-shrunk, so that its first encounter with hot water won't cause it to pucker and distort the edge of your cloth. Check too that the dye in your main fabric is fast, so it won't run and ruin the effect of a white or pale-coloured border.

YOU WILL NEED

FABRIC

SEWING THREAD OR MACHINE EMBROIDERY THREAD (SEE METHOD, STEP 4)

SEWING MACHINE WITH CLOSE ZIG-ZAG OR SATIN-STITCH FACILITY

COLOURED PENCIL AND RULER

SHARP DRESSMAKER'S SHEARS

EMBROIDERY SCISSORS

DUST-REPELLENT SPRAY (OPTIONAL)

1 You may be able to use just one large piece of fabric. But if you have difficulty in finding a fabric wide enough for your table, buy twice the required length and cut the fabric in half crosswise. Cut one piece in half lengthwise and then seam the half widths to each side of the remaining piece. In this way, the seam will not run down the centre of the cloth.

2 Mark the triangles around the edge, using a sharp coloured pencil in a shade close to that of the fabric. Start by marking diamond shapes at the corners, then work out how many triangles you can fit along each edge. To find the ideal size for the triangles, draw the shaped edge to a smaller scale on graph paper. (Depending on the size of the cloth, you might find that

you need a slightly broader or more angular triangle on the short sides.)

3 If you are not used to satin stitching, practise on a scrap of fabric before you begin stitching the tablecloth since it is important that the stitching is smooth, flat, and even. Set your machine to a

close zig-zag (satin), and stitch around the marked, uncut edge with the feeder teeth in the working position. Begin and end sewing with a few backstitches, with the machine on its straight-stitch setting. You may find that at the points and corners you need to alter the width setting, but the stitch length should remain the same throughout.

4 If you find that a close stitch setting tends to clog your sewing machine, adjust to a slightly wider setting and machine a second row over the first. (Machine embroidery cotton passes through the needle more smoothly and is less likely to clog than sewing cotton. It also has a looser twist and therefore covers the fabric more effectively, but

it should nevertheless be possible to achieve a good result with normal sewing thread.)

5 When you have finished stitching, cut out the zig-zag edge, cutting as close to the stitching as possible. Go around the edge a second time with embroidery scissors, carefully trimming any loose threads.

6 As an alternative to zig-zag stitching, if your fabric is not prone to fraying and you don't plan to use the tablecloth too often, you could simply cut out the zig-zag edge using pinking shears, as we did on our tablecloth.

7 To protect the cloth from marks, you might like to treat it with a proprietary dust repellent spray.

CHAIR COVERS

Homely and simple in their early incarnations, loose covers (slip covers) soon became more elaborate, and were valued just as highly for their looks as their function, being removed only for very special occasions.

Loose covers have been a common furnishing item since Tudor times but were particularly popular during the eighteenth and early nineteenth centuries when they were known as case covers. These versatile items, commonly made up in fresh-looking checked or striped cotton, served several purposes: they protected precious fabrics from dust and from wear, disguised worn or dirty surfaces, and provided an easy way to change the look of a room.

Like so many other decorating tactics, loose covers are every bit as appealing and useful in our modern world as they were at any time in the past. So if your dining room needs cheering up, treat your upholstered chairs to a set of new clothes that attach with Velcro or ties so they can be removed easily for cleaning. Our covers have been made with a gusset, or welt, and box pleats, which give a more tailored look. For a similar, but slightly softer, more relaxed effect,

Flirty little box-pleated skirts make these chairs less serious and prettier, to suit the feminine mood of the dining room. The colour of the leaves matches the green in the check of the tablecloth.

make a simple version of the same idea, consisting only of a strip of fabric gathered around a piece of the same material cut to fit the chair's seat. A length of piping inserted between the seat and border would add a bit of detail, but it's not necessary. In terms of length, make your gathered cover short to look like a flirty frill, or longer to give the effect of a graceful skirt.

To cover a stool in a similar way, simply sew the border in a continuous length, without leaving slits to fit around a chair's back. Or use this technique to make a charming fitted tablecloth with the look of a loose cover – another device borrowed from the Georgian era, when case covers were used on all kinds of furniture including tables.

<u>YOU WILL NEED</u>

PAPER FOR TEMPLATES, SUCH AS BROWN
WRAPPING PAPER OR WALL LINING PAPER

FABRIC

MATCHING SEWING THREAD

VELCRO, 1.5CM (⅝IN) WIDE (BOTH STRIPS
SEW-ON)

You may have to adapt your covers slightly to suit the individual design of your dining chairs, in particular the shaping and fit of the chair legs, but this basic method will apply to many styles of upholstered dining chair.

Start by making a paper pattern of the surface of the chair seat, to the point where the seat cover will meet the side gusset. Extend the shape for a further 9cm (3½in) at the back, to make a flap of fabric to tuck down behind the chair seat and back; then add a 12mm (½in) seam allowance all around. Mark on the pattern the points at each side at which the back flap begins and transfer to the fabric when cutting out – these are the points at which the seam joining the top to the side gusset ends.

Decide on the ideal depth of gusset for your chair, bearing in mind that it is the gusset strip that meets in a Velcro join at the side back of the chair; the gusset should extend down the side of the chair to the point at which the base meets the legs. Measure around the edge of the chair to find the finished length of the gusset. Add 2.5cm (1in) to the depth, for seam allowances, and 7.5cm (3in) to the length, for turnings and overlap.

Decide on the finished depth of the box-pleated valance – the ideal depth will depend on the height of your chairs and the shape of the legs. Add 3.5cm (1¼in) to the depth for seam allowance and turnings.

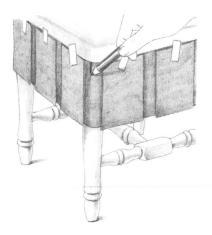

The arrangement of the pleats is again a matter of personal preference, and depends partly on the shape of your chairs. On the chairs featured here, there are three box pleats to each side, with spaces in between. Each pleat takes up its own width, plus a further two widths of fabric, so you will require a strip the length of the gusset strip, plus a further two times the pleat width for each pleat. In order to decide how wide to make the pleats, how far apart to space them, how to turn the edge attractively around the corners, and how deep to make the pleated edge, experiment with a strip of paper, which is pleated and held in place around the chair base with masking tape. Mark this with a pencil and then use it as a pattern when you are forming the pleats.

1 Pin, baste, and stitch the cover top to the side gusset, taking 12mm(½in) seam allowances. The gusset strip should extend beyond the cover top on one side by a length sufficient to run around the back leg on that side, plus a 12mm (½in) turning. On the other side, the gusset should be long enough to run along the back of the chair and overlap the other end by 5cm (2in) plus 12mm (½in) for a turning.

2 Neaten the raw edges around the back extensions of the gusset strip (along the top and bottom and the short side edges). Fold under the top edges at each end, making 12mm (½in) turnings, and herringbone stitch (blind catchstitch) in place (see page 17). Also neaten, turn, and herringbone stitch the side edges of the back extensions, and then make a double 1cm (⅜in) turning and hem along the back flap of the cover (the edge that will be tucked between the seat and chair back).

3 Turn under a double 1cm (⅜in) hem along the lower edge of the valance. Using either a coloured pencil or a dressmaker's marking pencil, mark the position of the pleats along the edge, on the right side of the fabric, making small vertical lines down for 12mm (½in) to mark the placement lines. The placement lines should be spaced two pleat widths apart. As a guide to positioning the pleats, use the paper pattern you made when measuring up.

4 For each pleat, bring the two placement lines to meet, with wrong sides together. Baste and stitch a vertical line running down from the raw, top edge for 2.5cm (1in), as shown on the left of the diagram below. Find the centre of the pleat by lightly folding, and bring this fold to meet the stitched line, flattening it out and forming the box pleat effect, with an equal amount of pleat at each side of the inner stitched line. Pin and baste the pleat along the top edge, to hold it, as shown on the centre pleat below. Now stitch along the basted line, just inside the 12mm (½in) seam allowance, as shown on the right-hand pleat.

5 When you have finished forming the pleats, lightly press the valance, pressing in the pleats, before attaching the valance to the gusset.

6 Taking a 12mm (½in) seam allowance, attach the pleated valance to the gusset strip. Neaten the side edges; turn under the side edges of the gusset/valance making a 12mm (½in) turning at each side edge and herringbone stitching it in place. Stitch a strip of Velcro to each overlapping edge of the gusset strip, stitching one side of the Velcro to the wrong side of the overlapping edge, and stitching the other half to the right side of the underlying piece, to match it.

7 Fit the cover over the chair, tucking in the back flap, and pressing the overlapping edge to close it.

NAPKINS

There is a much wider range of suitable fabrics to choose from in the stores than there are napkins, so making your own napkins is a great way to imbue your dining room with your own style; it is also much more economical. Choose a washable and not too lightweight fabric and simply cut it into appropriately sized squares and hem the edges.

Without picking up a needle, however, you can acquire huge cotton napkins in enchanting designs simply by casting your shopping net a little wider. Cotton headscarves are widely available in plain colours, cheeky spots, and an ever-changing range of attractive designs.

Provençal scarves, made from the traditional fabric of southern France, are particularly pretty and practical; they come in an abundance of different colours, patterns, and sizes and are ideal for picnics and informal meals. Another good choice is large, old-fashioned men's handkerchiefs.

Another advantage of buying napkins this way is that you never have to take them in matching sets. You may want four or six that are the same, of course, but you could also choose a single design and have one napkin in each colourway, perhaps allocating a different colour to every family member.

NAPKIN RINGS

Another way to change the look of your table is with napkin rings. Make your own instantly by tying your napkins up with a length of ribbon, cord, braid, or lace. Change it according to the occasion: gold or seasonally embroidered ribbon for Christmas, velvet or grosgrain for formal dinners, and coloured cord or tape for friendly suppers and children's parties. You might like to colour-code each child's place.

Alternatively, use exquisite silk flowers; these often have a length of flexible wire wound into their stems, which you can twist loosely around each napkin. Here, too, you could put the same bloom or small posy at each place; or choose a selection of flowers, so that each napkin looks different. Or, do the same thing with garden

flowers, binding their stems with wire and a little wet cotton wool (cotton) to keep them looking fresh as the evening wears on.

For a much more casual look, slip the napkins through "scrunchies" (elasticated fabric hair bands) in plain colours and fabrics.

TOP LEFT To reinforce a spring-like colour theme, finish off your napkins with floppy bows in tender green and yellow, then tuck a sprig of fragrant herbs in each one.
TOP RIGHT Antique tray cloths and antimacassars make pretty serving or place mats, and they're often easier to find than conventional table linen in a similar condition. Napkins tied with organza bows give a contemporary look.
BOTTOM LEFT Use big blue neckerchiefs as napkins, and gather them into casual folds with strips of raffia.
BOTTOM RIGHT Fasten napkins with wired ribbon twisted into rosettes, then arranged in two-tone clusters that bring together the scheme's main colours.

LEFT Softly gathered loose covers with long self-ties look stylish against the hard surface and dramatic geometric pattern of the tiled floor in this French dining room.

OPPOSITE The formal use of a whimsical novelty vegetable wallpaper and fabric makes this formal dining room less serious. This type of rope-swagged curtain treatment was popular in the eighteenth century and the idea of double curtains comes from France. The deep aubergine colour is taken from the radishes in the vegetables. These are drawn in a manner characteristic of old engravings and therefore do not conflict with the sober period curtain treatment.

CHAPTER FOUR

Kitchens

When you consider the enormous range of fitted units and elaborate accessories available today, it's difficult to believe that the kitchen has only recently been considered a suitable area for decoration. Although this room has always been extremely important, until the start of the First World War no sensible household would spend unnecessary time and effort on it since it was essentially the domain of servants, and even ordinary families had at least one maid whose responsibilities included the preparation of meals. What's more, cooking was a greasy, smoky, sooty business, and extraneous trimmings only made extra work.

In contrast, today's kitchens tend to be gathering places for the family, often the heart and hub of a home. So many people nowadays live a less formal lifestyle and many find a dining room is not necessary, preferring a more casual approach to mealtimes.

The advent of the attractive fitted kitchen and the comparatively recent emphasis on comfort and decoration make the kitchen a much more social room. Often a kitchen might contain a play area so a toddler can keep his mother company.

This kitchen was inspired by the two red-and-white woven glasscloths made into a cushion on the pine chairs. The theme gives the pine furniture and white walls a contemporary look. All the accessories – the neckerchiefs as napkins, the dimity-print tea cosy, and the checked pinboard – were made or chosen to match the colour story. The white walls, with a small amount of stencilling above the fireplace recess, are a perfect foil for the red.

This cheerful breakfast setting has been largely improvised using elements intended for use in other ways. True to the spirit of the room, a waffle-weave tea towel was laid across the table's width so that it makes two place mats; the napkin is a cotton neckerchief.

Window treatments for the kitchen are most practical if kept to restrained fabric. Use styles like roller or roman blinds (shades) or single width curtains, avoiding fussy trimmings, festoons (balloon shades), frills or lace.

Keep it simple and make sure curtain fabric and chair seat covers are removable and washable. It's a good idea to use a fire-retardant fabric if possible.

In our kitchen, we've looked to classic tea towels for design inspiration. The cushion covers, the place mats, and the curtains are made from actual tea towels, while the pinboard, the tea cosy, and the shelf trimmings were chosen because they fit in well with the look. Copy our ideas and treat plain, checked, or jacquard towels as if they were fabric – or choose traditional ones woven with the words LINEN or GLASS CLOTH. Our colour theme is red and white, but most tea towel designs are available in white with blue or green and sometimes in more unusual shades. If you want to use fabric instead, any cotton or linen woven in fresh, simple checks or stripes would give a similar effect. There is also a large range of patterned tea towels, some of them fairly quirky, that could suit any number of decorating themes.

If you like the idea of a kitchen decorating scheme centred around a theme, there is a wide variety of subjects to choose from. For a kitchen, an obvious theme is food – fruit, vegetables, fish, or seafood. The farmyard is also a strong theme for a country kitchen. Find a novelty print fabric that features your chosen theme and pick out of it a dominant colour around which you can coordinate all the elements of your decorating scheme: moss green for vegetables or straw yellow for hens and poultry. You can then begin to collect accessories featuring your theme: oven gloves and aprons, tea towels, framed prints, and an assortment of china to display on the dresser.

CAFÉ CURTAINS

Fresh and cheerful to look at, café curtains are also extremely practical since they provide privacy yet admit a considerable amount of light through the top part of the window. They can be used in bedrooms, bathrooms, and living rooms, but the natural habitat of the domestic café curtain is the kitchen, as they are easy to take down and wash. Also, the small windows common in kitchens suit this simple design better than larger ones. Although café curtains can be hung any distance from the top of a window, the rod or pole that supports them is usually positioned centrally.

To create a charming and distinctive curtain that requires very little time or money, make it out of stitched-together tea towels. Finished along both sides so they don't need hemming, these look best in traditional tea-towel designs. We've chosen tiny checks, but you'd get the same look with a striped pattern or one woven with the classic LINEN or GLASS CLOTH emblem along the sides. If your tastes are even simpler, go for plain-coloured towels.

The time-honoured way of hanging café curtains is with rings. To make this unlined curtain presentable from both sides, attach the rings to the top of the fabric rather than using heading tape. Another option is to insert brass eyelets along the edge of the fabric, as we have done on our curtain. Eyelets are available in several sizes; large ones might actually be bigger than the thickness of your curtain rod, which could then just slip through the eyelets without recourse to rings. If that's not possible, use cord ties or fit rings through the eyelets and hang these on the rod in the usual way. A curtain hung with cord ties or rings would, of course, be a little longer than one with the pole threaded through eyelets, so this option would be better if your curtain is falling a little short.

In place of standard rings, we've hung our café curtains from rope ties – matching or contrasting tape, cord, or ribbon would each give a slightly different look. This method allows you to adjust the ties according to the curtain length required.

YOU WILL NEED

WOODEN DOWEL AND BRASS FIXINGS
TEA TOWELS OR TEA TOWEL FABRIC – THE
COMBINED WIDTH SHOULD BE ONE-AND-A-
HALF TIMES THE WIDTH OF THE DOWEL
MATCHING SEWING THREAD
EYELET TOOL AND BRASS EYELETS, 2.5CM
(1IN) IN DIAMETER – USED FOR SAILMAKING
AND AVAILABLE FROM CHANDLERS
CORD, FOR TIES (OPTIONAL)

Threading your curtain pole directly through large brass eyelets gives a slightly more tailored look, with a smart stand-up heading at the top.

1 Lay the widths of fabric together lengthwise, lapping the long edges and stitch together, using a machine straight stitch. This sort of seam makes the curtains look good from both sides.

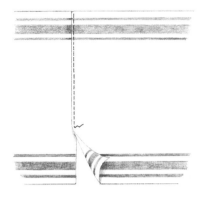

2 Using a pencil, make vertical marks for eyelets at regular intervals – we used an average of between four and five eyelets per towel width. The lines on the fabric will act as horizontal guidelines when you are marking the points. Punch brass eyelets into the curtain at the marked points, using the eyelet tool.

3 Fix the curtain pole in position, either slotting the pole through the eyelets first, or threading lengths of cord through the eyelets and tying them in reef knots (square knots, in which you take right over left and then left over right) at the top of the pole.

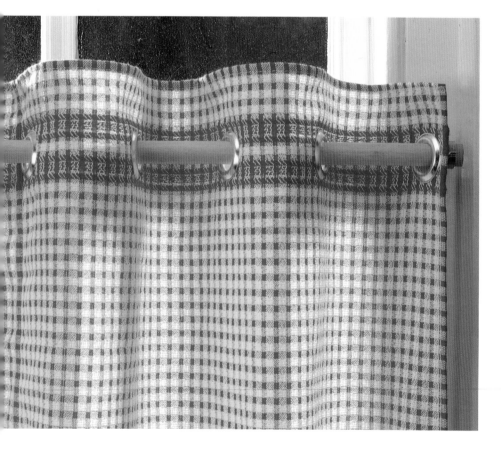

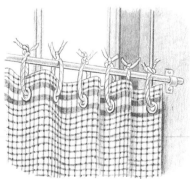

KITCHEN CUPBOARDS

Kitchen-cupboard doors can present a variety of knotty problems, both decorative and practical. When you move into a new home, you often find units that are perfectly serviceable, but just not to your taste, and even the doors on units you originally chose eventually become scuffed and sad-looking – or you simply tire of them. In tiny kitchens, cupboard doors can be a real hazard, maliciously banging heads and making it uncomfortable for more than one person to work in the room at a time.

One good solution to these problems is to remove the doors altogether and replace them with fabric. Below the counter, install simple curtains made of cotton or linen, which are easy to wash. Plain white or cream fabric will give a lovely French-farmhouse feeling to the room, while a colourful check, stripe, or print can add drama; for ours, we've used a rustic vine-and-leaf pattern whose mood harmonizes with our homely tea-towel theme.

Measure the run of your counter, and allow enough fabric for the finished curtains to be about 1½ times this width – more fullness would be inappropriate in a kitchen. Hang the curtain on wire stretched between hooks, or from a thin length of brass tubing or wooden dowel. You can either use rings or run the rod straight through a casing at the top.

Above counter level, some kind of blind would work best – a conventional roller design, or a roll-up blind, which simply hangs flat from a pole batten at the top, and rolls up from the bottom (see Garden Rooms chapter, page 123).

If head clearance isn't a problem, and your doors are difficult to remove, cover them completely with lightweight curtains gathered onto wire at top and bottom.

Exactly the same technique can be used for disguising internal glazed doors. Simply fix a gathered curtain to each side; as with cupboard doors, there is very little stitchery involved, just casings at top and bottom. Slip lengths of wire through these to hang your curtains, which are then very simple to remove for washing.

A pretty sprigged-cotton skirt conceals the cluttered shelves behind. When you want low-level curtains to go around a corner, use expandable wire rather than a fixed rod. If there is no cupboard-door frame under your work surface, an extra hook fixed into the underside at each corner will anchor the fabric in position.

TEA COSY

Add another personal touch to your kitchen by making your own tea cosy – as well offering an infinite range of materials and shapes for you to choose from, sewing this item yourself allows you to make it much bigger and thicker than any similar item you could buy.

The obvious choice for a covering fabric would be one that matches other things in the room – the curtains or tablecloth perhaps – or that bears out a decorating theme. Alternatively, this would be another inspired use for tea-towel cotton or linen, though for this purpose, an all-over pattern would be better than one with a border.

Or choose something surprising like a flowery chintz, a sophisticated dog's-tooth check, or a winsome nursery print, all of which are traditionally used elsewhere. For a witty finish, sew a tassel on the top, or a serious-looking upholstery fringe around the bottom. The only requirement is that everything you use should be washable. Use closely woven cotton for the lining, and dacron or polyester wadding (batting) for the padding. Measure your teapot and allow plenty of extra room so that the cosy won't be too tight a fit. For maximum insulation, add as much padding as you can.

YOU WILL NEED

2 COORDINATING PRINTED COTTON FABRICS
– ONE FOR THE OUTER COVER, AND ONE FOR
THE LINING AND BINDING
MATCHING SEWING THREAD
MEDIUM WEIGHT POLYESTER OR DACRON
WADDING (BATTING)

1 First make a paper pattern for the tea cosy. On a piece of cartridge paper or brown wrapping paper, draw a rectangle big enough to cover your teapot; one measuring 30 x 28.7cm (12 x 11½in) will fit a standard pot. Using a saucer to mark the shape, round off the corners at each end of one larger side – this will be the top. Cut out the paper shape and use this to cut two shapes from the outer fabric, two from the lining fabric, and two from wadding (batting). Trim 12mm (½in) from the bottom (straight) edge of both wadding pieces.

2 Take a piece of outer fabric and one of lining and, with right sides facing outwards, sandwich a piece of wadding between them, aligning the top (curved) edges of all three layers. Pin and baste the pieces together up one side, along the top and back down, and then stitch, taking a 6mm (¼in) seam allowance. Repeat, to make a second padded section.

3 On the lower edge of each section of the cosy, fold the front fabric over the wadding and turn in the raw edge of the lining fabric so that it cannot be seen from the front. Slipstitch (see page 17) along the folded edge.

4 With the tea cosy right side out, pin and baste the front and back sections together and stitch around the sides and top, along the first stitching lines.

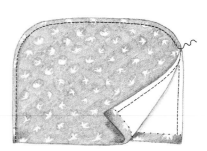

5 Make a 2.5cm (1in) wide strip of bias binding (see page 130), to run around the sides and top of the cosy, plus extra for the hanging loop. Fold in and press the long raw edges of the binding, so that they almost meet at the centre, on the wrong side.

6 Make a hanging loop by folding a 4cm (1½in) length of the folded bias binding in half lengthwise and stitching close to the edge. Fold the length of binding in half and sew it to the top of the cosy, with the raw ends even with the raw edge of the cosy.

7 Unfold the edge of the binding on one side and pin the binding around the sides and top of the cosy, with raw edges even. Stitch along the fold line of the bias binding. At the bottom edge turn both raw ends of the binding neatly to the wrong side.

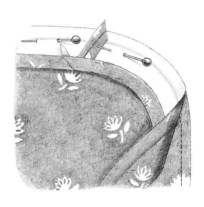

8 Bring the bias binding over the raw edge of the cosy and slipstitch (see page 17) the folded edge of the binding to the other side of the cosy, just covering the machine stitching.

The main section of our tea cosy was made from cotton dress fabric in a cheerful sprigged pattern. As a coordinating detail, we lined and piped it with a dotty print.

FLANGED CUSHION

For a simple, elegant change from ordinary cushions, make up a collection of covers with plain flat borders, called flanges. Rather like the daytime equivalent of an Oxford pillow case, flanged cushion covers suit a variety of decorating styles and fabrics. One effective and easy idea is to make covers from pairs of border-print cotton scarves, handkerchiefs or, as we have done, tea towels, whose design is ideally suited to the flange construction. Provençal scarves, made of traditional fabric from southern France, feature this type of decoration in clear primary or subtle subdued colours, and several different sizes. Men's handkerchiefs with suitably checked or bordered designs also work well; standard ones are only about 40cm (16in) square, so they would make quite small cushions, but you can often buy an old-fashioned version up to 50–60cm (20–24in) in gentlemen's outfitters. Another possibility is to use exquisitely hem-stitched white handkerchiefs to make more feminine cushions for the bedroom.

To make a single flange, sew the two squares together around the outside before you make the line of stitching that defines the border. To make a double flange, which involves even less work, leave the outside edges open – their hemmed or rolled edges will give your cover a neat, professional finish.

The tea towels we used had a bordered edge which converted easily into the flanged edge of the cushion. There are various ways you could make it. One quick and easy option, described below, is to use a washable cushion pad and stitch it into the cushion, then simply put the entire cushion in the washing machine (following the washing instructions for the pillow exactly). Alternatively, use a tea towel for the front, but make the back from a similar fabric, with a zip inserted across the centre.

We've used jacquard-weave French tea towels for both cushions. The large one is made from two stitched together, and the other from one, folded in half and stitched, with a zip added.

YOU WILL NEED

2 TEA TOWELS

MATCHING SEWING THREAD

WASHABLE CUSHION PAD OR PILLOW

1 Lay the pillow centrally on top of one of the tea towels. Using the pillow as a guide, draw a rectangle on the right side of one so that when the back and front of the cover are stitched together, the pillow will be firmly held.

2 Set the pillow to one side. With wrong sides together and the edges even, pin, baste, and stitch the tea towels together along two long sides and one short side, close to the edge. Also stitch along the marked inner line on the same three sides.

3 Insert the pillow into the cover, and stitch the remaining short side, again stitching along the outer edge and the marked inner line.

PINBOARD

Endlessly useful for messages, shopping lists, calendars, appointment cards, postcards, and children's drawings, pinboards in their most common form are made from an unassuming material such as cork tiles or are covered with plain baize or felt. For a cheerful change, make your pinboard out of a single sheet of cork or fibreboard, then cover it with a printed fabric that suits the style of the room. We've used small checks, but you could choose ticking stripes to suit a smart, contemporary scheme, or cabbage roses for a classic English country look.

Another, very traditional version of the notice board is made from a similar material and also covered with fabric, but items are tucked behind lengths of tape or braid criss-crossed over the surface in a trellis pattern. The simplest way to anchor the tape or braid is with a brass drawing pin (thumbtack) or brightly coloured pinhead inserted at each point where the tapes cross.

SHELF EDGINGS

For an old-fashioned country look, fix pretty edging to some of your shelves. In the kitchen, larder, or dining room, trim open shelves on the wall or at the top of a dresser with a length of cotton lace, pompon fringe, or narrow broderie anglaise (eyelet) – or try wide ribbon (straight, or gathered like our mini-check pattern) in a bright colour, a woven pattern, or a tartan design. Tack it to the front edge with thin, almost invisible nails, or use bold brass drawing pins (thumbtacks) that become part of the effect. Alternatively, glue the edging in place, applying the glue lightly so you can remove the trim for washing. In the kitchen, it's important that any trimming you choose is either washable or so inexpensive that you won't mind replacing it when it is past its best.

Edging shelves like this works well in lots of situations; use lace inside a wardrobe, a linen press, or a glass-fronted cupboard. In the nursery, one of the delightful woven ribbons designed for babies and children would suit shelves that hold clothing or small toys.

In the nineteenth century, shelves in public rooms (and especially mantel shelves) often had their own fabric covers in the form of a valance or a lambrequin. Adapt this rather formal look by decorating shelves in the living room or study with heavy cord, braid, or gimp. Or borrow a trick from canny Victorian chatelaines and attach along the edge of every bookshelf a length of straight fringe that is deep enough to brush the top of each book on the shelf below as it is removed – not only does it add decoration but it also dusts the volumes automatically.

Woven shelf edgings can suit a variety of different decorating styles. Bright tape – plain or striped – looks graphic and bold; gathered ribbon or lace has a wholesome, country feeling; while pompons add a touch of individuality.

OPPOSITE An upholstered chair or sofa adds a note of comfort to any kitchen, and this chair's rounded shape and frilled edge contribute some softness to the room's clean lines. A cheerful, bright atmosphere has been created with the use of yellow, white, and blue, and the unusual blue-checked china is echoed in the chair covering.

LEFT Use jute fan edging to turn a hardworking adjustable shelf system into a stylish kitchen display area. The undyed natural texture of the jute coordinates with the neutral bold check and echoes the other natural materials in the kitchen.

The design of this pretty, rural kitchen, with its comfortable sofa, frilled cushions, doorway curtain, and matching wallpaper, makes few visual concessions to the many practical functions it fulfils. Without the flagstone floor and the softwood table and chairs, the scheme would work equally well in an urban living room. It is a family room for convivial, informal gatherings as well as a workplace.

CHAPTER FIVE

Bedrooms

The bedroom is the most personal, intimate room in the house – a refuge from the hurly-burly of family life, a haven for relaxation, and a private domain whose design reflects its owner's tastes and habits.

Setting aside special, private places for sleeping and dressing has not always been the custom, however. Until the eighteenth century, the bedchambers of the wealthy and aristocratic were essentially reception rooms, where friends, political allies, diplomats, business contacts, and other worthies were entertained. Beds were huge and ornate, designed not for the comfort and delight of the occupant, but to impress those who were welcomed from within their opulent drapes. In more modest homes, where there simply was not the space to set aside a special area for such limited use, the inhabitants tended to live, sleep, cook, eat, and bathe in the same room. For the last two hundred years or so, however, most households have been organized very much like modern dwellings, with separate quarters set aside for sleeping.

The design scheme for a bedroom will probably need to respect this main function by providing a calm, restful atmosphere. One advantage is that many of the pedestrian considerations that can be

To guarantee a restful, harmonious scheme, stick to natural colours and textures. In this sophisticated bedroom, we've used snowy linen, taupe-and-white cotton checks and stripes, undyed coir and jute, with touches of wood, clay, and raffia. The pale hues are not as impractical as they seem; almost all the surfaces and materials are washable, from the bedclothes and hangings to the cushions and the eggshell paint that is used on the woodwork.

Add a stylish trim to plain cushions with a border of fringe or jute rope. For a touch of drama, stitch a coordinating tassel (small and subtle or fat and fabulous) to each corner.

limiting in a living room or kitchen do not apply here – floors don't have to be washable or particularly hardwearing, surfaces aren't at constant risk from spilled food and drink, and seating is unlikely to be subjected to heavy use. This means that, with the exception of the bed, furnishing elements can be chosen more on aesthetic than practical grounds – an exciting prospect in a room that offers tremendous scope for decorating with textiles. In addition to conventional soft-furnishing items such as curtains and cushions, you can take full advantage of the exquisite bedlinen and accessories currently available to help you create exactly the look you want. Choose traditional blankets or plump duvets, teamed with matching sets of sheets, pillowslips, and duvet covers. Some ranges even include curtains, cushions, lampshades, tablecloths, and fabric so you can coordinate your room completely if you want to. Antique textiles can also look wonderful here.

For our bedroom, we've combined the contemporary feel of subtle, natural colours and textures and simple geometric patterns with a furnishing style that takes its inspiration from the past. To achieve a similar effect, choose a decorating palette of warm whites, creams, and beiges.

Alternatively, use exactly the same elements and simply change the colours. To create a rich, exotic mood, base your scheme around autumn hues – drape the bed and the windows with deep gold or russet, give the walls a colour wash of soft terracotta, and use accent shades of cinnamon, olive, and saffron.

MOCK FOUR-POSTER

Heavily draped four-poster beds dominated the sleeping chambers of all but the poorest families in Europe for hundreds of years, from the early medieval period until the Victorian age. Like many other household textiles, the elaborate hangings were to some degree a status symbol, but curtained beds were also of great practical value. Their function was to protect their occupants against icy draughts, but they fulfilled another role in offering a modicum of privacy at a time when, even in the most aristocratic households, it was common for several people or couples to share a room.

Few of us today possess a four-poster, but gracefully draped bed curtains can still give a timeless allure to any bedroom. To achieve this look without bedposts, hang generously gathered lengths of fabric (using conventional tape and hooks) from curtain poles or tracks fixed directly into ceiling joists above the bed. Choose a plain, reversible material, or a printed one, perhaps self-lined so it will look just as nice from inside. If you are happy with just the look of a draped bed, and don't require the curtains to draw, hang them from eyelets in wooden battens fixed into the ceiling. An even easier solution is to staple the fabric to the wood, but this makes the curtains awkward to remove for cleaning. Conceal any hardware behind a short, self-fabric pelmet (cornice). Beds that project into the room should have curtains down both sides and across the bottom, while those that are tucked in a corner will require only two runs of fabric. In a small, narrow room, position your bed across the width at one end, and fix a single curtain in front of it.

For our mock four-poster, we used antique linen sheets hung from curtain tracks attached to four pieces of timber fixed to the ceiling. (Crisp new white ones would give a similar effect.) Eight curtains were used – two for each side. To conceal the timber, a pelmet (cornice) in the same antique linen was stuck to it with Velcro. The pelmet was attached to the outside edges of the timber frame, and the curtains hung from the inside edges.

If however, your ceiling is very high, or you prefer a simpler effect, you could arrange a length of soft material across the head of the bed

– either draped over a short wooden, brass, or iron pole at right angles to the bedhead, or caught in a large hook; both of these can be fixed into the ceiling or the wall above the pillows. Your fabric should fall to the floor on each side of the bed – if it threatens to get in the way, anchor it around a pair of curtain bosses or tie-back hooks positioned next to the mattress on each side.

Whether your bed hangings are elaborate or simple, they should coordinate with the soft furnishings elsewhere in the room. You could choose pretty cotton lace or muslin for your bed drapes, and use the same fabric at the window.

YOU WILL NEED

7.5 X 5CM (3 X 2IN) TIMBER BATTENS
FIXING SCREWS
CURTAIN TRACK, HEADING TAPE, AND HOOKS
(OPTIONAL, FOR CURTAINS THAT CAN BE
DRAWN SHUT)
VELCRO, WITH ONE STRIP SELF-ADHESIVE
AND ONE STRIP SEW-ON
LINEN OR COTTON SHEETS – 4 DOUBLE
SHEETS FOR THE CURTAINS AND 2 SINGLE
SHEETS FOR THE PELMET (CORNICE)
BEIGE WEBBING, 5CM (2IN) WIDE
STAPLE GUN (OPTIONAL)

MEASURING

First measure the length of your bed (with bedding), and cut two pieces of timber to this length plus an extra 7.5cm (3in). Cut two pieces to the width of the bed.

For the curtains, the sheets are used as they are, without cutting or hemming. Measure from the frame once it is in place, to ensure that the sheets are long enough to reach the floor. (Be sure to measure from the Velcro or track.) Any excess can pool onto the floor, adding to the luxurious look of the drapes.

For the pelmet (cornice), cut two side strips and two head/foot strips from the single sheets. They should be the same length as the timber, and the desired depth of the pelmet, plus 2.5cm (1in) on all edges.

ASSEMBLING THE FRAMEWORK

1 Screw the timber battens into the ceiling joists. If the ceiling joists are not in the ideal position, and if you have access to the ceiling from above, perhaps from a loft (attic) space, you can fix exra noggings betwen joists and then screw the timber framework to the noggings.

2 If you want the curtains to draw shut, mount curtain track inside the timber frame. If you want the hangings to remain permanently open, attach eight 40cm (16in) strips of Velcro to the inside lower edge of the frame on each side of every corner; alternatively, use a staple gun to staple the hook side of the Velcro in place.

3 For the pelmet (cornice), attach a continuous strip of Velcro along the top edge of the outside of the frame along both sides and the foot, continuing it right around the corners. At the head of the bed (assuming it is against the wall), attach the Velcro to the inside of the frame.

MAKING THE PELMET

1 Turn under and stitch a double 12mm (½in) hem along all four sides of each of the four pelmet strips.

2 Machine stitch Velcro to the top edge of each pelmet strip, stitching it to the right side of the side/foot strips and to the wrong side of the head strip.

3 Fold the Velcro over to the other side of each strip. Attach the side/foot strips to the Velcro on the outside of the bed frame. Attach the head strip to the Velcro on the inside of the frame, where it will cover the top of the curtains.

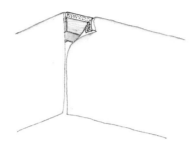

4 Cut two lengths of webbing, each at least twice the depth of the pelmet. Trim the ends to angled points. At the centre stitch a piece of Velcro across the width of the webbing.

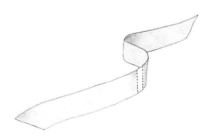

5 Hang the doubled webbing at the corners at the foot of the frame.

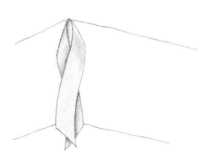

MAKING THE CURTAINS

1 For each of the four curtains, if you are using Velcro rather than track, cut a strip of the stitch-on side of the Velcro to the finished width of the curtain (ie, the length of the corresponding Velcro that is attached to the inside of the frame).

2 Pleat the top edge of the curtain by hand to the finished width, pinning the pleats in place. Machine stitch the Velcro to the wrong side of the curtain along the pleated edge. Fold the Velcro edge over to the right side of the curtain (the side facing out of the frame) and attach it to the strips of Velcro on the inside of the frame.

3 If you are using track instead of Velcro, stitch curtain heading tape to the right side of the sheets, setting the tape just below the top edge. Insert hooks, and hang on the track.

BED VALANCE

Designed to cover the base of the bed and give it a finished look, a valance can be frilled (known as a dust ruffle in the US) or it can be tailored and straight with pleats at the corners (a bed skirt in the US). To add interest to a straight valance, cut out a shaped edge; we've chosen a stepped, castellated design that suits the geometric pattern of our fabric, but scallops or zig-zags would work just as well. As with the tablecloth on page 41, you could use this shape to establish a design motif for the room, repeating it on the curtain pelmet (cornice), perhaps, or on the skirt of a loose-covered chair. If you have a divan base that extends almost to the floor, you will want your valance to cover it completely. If your bed is on legs, however, try making your valance several inches shorter for a different effect. The fabric you choose for a tailored valance like this one should be fairly substantial, but don't waste expensive material on the panel that goes under the mattress – use curtain lining or sheeting instead.

For an instant and stylish way to conceal your bed base, simply buy a large flat sheet that matches or contrasts with your bedlinen (or a bedspread in plain cotton, linen, or lace), and place it under the mattress so that it falls over the base and onto the floor.

YOU WILL NEED

SOFT FURNISHING FABRIC (FOR THE VISIBLE PART OF THE VALANCE)

MATCHING SEWING THREAD

PLAIN COTTON OR COTTON/POLYESTER LINING OR SHEETING FABRIC (FOR THE SECTION UNDER THE MATTRESS)

STRAIGHT BINDING TAPE, 12MM (½IN) WIDE

MEASURING

Measure the length and width of the bed base. (If the base has very rounded corners, you can shape the valance to them at a later stage, but for the present, measure the maximum dimensions.) The central portion of the valance is a rectangle to these dimensions; for reasons of economy, the centre, which is not visible, is cut from plain lining or sheeting fabric, but to avoid this fabric being seen, there is a 15cm (6in) deep frame of the main fabric all around the rectangle. Because it is joined to the rectangle with 12mm (½in) seams, cut a rectangle of lining fabric to the bed base measurements less 30cm (12in) each way; and four strips of main fabric, all 17.5cm (7in) deep – two to the width of the bed plus 2.5cm (1in) and two to the length plus 2.5cm (1in).

The depth of the straight border (without castellations) seen here is 20cm (8in), though you may wish to adjust this to suit the proportions of your bed. Cut strips of main fabric to this depth measurement plus 2.5cm (1in), joining them until you have a piece equal to the width of the bed plus twice the length plus 5cm (2in).

There are eight tabs/castellations down the sides of this bed, and six at the bottom, the spaces in between being roughly the same width as the tabs. The tabs seen here are 7.5cm (3in) deep and 13.5cm (5¼in) wide, but again you may wish to make your tabs slightly longer or shorter, depending on the proportions of your bed. For each tab, cut a piece of fabric to the desired width plus 2.5cm (1in) and twice the desired length, plus 2.5cm (1in). If your fabric has a noticeable pattern, the tabs will need to be pattern-matched as they are cut out.

Alternatively, cut the valance to a depth that includes the castellations plus seam allowance – here this would be 30cm (12in) – and then cut a castellated edge from it. For this method, you need to cut two identical pieces for each side of the valance, as they are sewn together (see step 8).

1 First prepare the central section of the valance – the base cover. With right sides together, stitch one of the short strips of main fabric to one of the short edges of the lining fabric rectangle, taking a 12mm (½in) seam allowance; leave 15cm (6in) extra at each end, and begin and finish stitching 12mm (½in) in from the edges. Join the other short strip to the other short edge, and the two long strips to the two long edges of the rectangle in the same manner.

2 At each corner, fold the two ends of the border strips into a mitre. Press along the fold line, trim away excess fabric, and stitch the mitred seams.

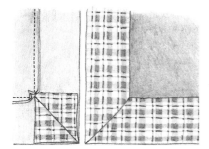

3 If the corners of the bottom of the bed are rounded, lay a plate with a matching curve on each corner of the framed fabric in turn. Using a pencil, mark a curve on the fabric, and then trim along the curved line.

4 To prepare each tab, fold the strip of fabric in half crosswise, with right sides together, and stitch the side seams, taking 12mm (½in) seam allowances. Turn the tab right side out and press. Zig-zag stitch the raw edges at the end of the tab together.

5 Turn under a double 12mm (½in) hem at each short end of the valance strip and stitch. Using pins or tailor's chalk, mark the positions of the sides and bottom of the bed, and the centre points along each, on the lower and upper edges of the valance. Lay the tabs flat on the right side of the valance, with the neatened edges of the tabs matching the raw lower edge of the valance and with the checks or other pattern matching. Position a tab at each end of each side, and space the others at regular intervals between them. The distance of the tab from each end should be half the distance between tabs. Baste and then stitch each of the tabs in position, taking 12mm (½in) seam allowances.

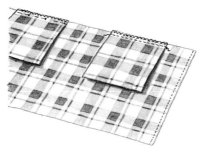

6 Still on the right side of the valance, pin and stitch straight binding tape along the raw lower edge, also covering the raw edges of the tabs, so the binding forms a hem along the edge.

7 Turn the fabric to the wrong side for 12mm (½in) and sew the hem, catching the straight binding tape to the back of the main fabric.

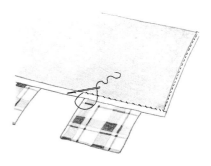

8 If you are cutting a castellated edge from a wider valance strip, instead of sewing on tabs, use the check pattern, if there is one, as a basis for the size and position of the castellations. Cut out two pieces of fabric for each side, then stitch the fabric pairs together, with right sides facing and raw edges even, along the castellated edge and the ends. Turn the valance right side out, and press. Baste the raw, top edge together.

9 With right sides together and raw edges even, pin, baste, and stitch the valance border to the base cover, using the positioning marks as guidelines.

TIE-ON CURTAINS

In their simplest sewn form, curtains have no heading tape – plain ties or tabs fasten them to their pole. (This style only works with a curtain pole or rod; track requires conventional heading tape and hooks.) To reinforce their relaxed, uncontrived look, make your curtains in a lightweight cotton or linen so that sunlight can filter through. Similarly, this style looks best without elaborate tie-backs or ornate hardware.

Make self-fabric ties, or sew on some ties made of cord or strong ribbon instead. To anchor the outside edges of each curtain, position the last couple of ties outside the brackets that hold the pole in place. These curtains don't require quite as much fullness as those gathered onto heading tape; 1½ or 2 times the width of your window should be ample.

Our simple, lined curtain is tied to a pole with strips of the curtain fabric and has a self-pelmet (integral valance). The depth of the self-pelmet will depend on the proportions of your window – the pelmet seen here is approximately 25cm (10in) deep, to suit the tall window. Again because the window was tall and narrow, we used a single curtain (matched by another on the window at the other side of the bed).

YOU WILL NEED

MAIN CURTAIN FABRIC
MATCHING SEWING THREAD
LINING FABRIC
STRIP OF BUCKRAM, 10CM (4IN) WIDE
CURTAIN POLE

MEASURING

First measure the width of the curtain pole and the length of the drop from just below the pole to floor level. The main curtain fabric should be twice the width of the pole plus an allowance of 8cm (3in) for side turnings, and the length of the drop plus twice the desired depth of the pelmet, 2.5cm (1in) for the top turning, and a further 10cm (4in) for the bottom hem.

The lining fabric should be twice the width of the pole, and the length of the drop plus 2.5cm (1in) for the top turning and 6.5cm (2½in) for the bottom hem.

The width of the ties can again be varied to suit your fabric. Ours were each made from two strips of fabric, 5cm (2in) wide and 53.5cm (21in) long, which meant that their finished width was 2.5cm (1in) and each half of a tie was 25.5cm (10in) long.

You will also require a band of buckram to the width of the finished curtain.

1 Working down from the top raw edge of the curtain fabric, measure twice the depth of the pelmet plus 2.5cm (1in). Using tailor's chalk or a fine, sharp pencil, draw a horizontal line at this level on the wrong side of the fabric. Pin the band of buckram to the wrong side of the curtain with the top edge even with this line, leaving a 4cm (1½in) turning allowance at each side edge of the curtain. Lockstitch the buckram to the back of the curtain fabric using the technique shown on page 17, step 2.

2 Turn back and press a 4cm (1½in) turning down each side of the curtain, and a 2cm (¾in) turning down each side of the lining. Also turn under 2.5cm (1in) at the top raw edge of the lining fabric and press.

3 Fold the fabric to the back at the top so that the raw edge overlaps the strip of buckram by 2.5cm (1in). Baste just above the buckram in order to hold the fabric in place while you attach the curtain lining.

4 Turn, press and stitch a double 4cm (1½in) hem along the bottom of the lining fabric.

5 With the top, folded edge of the lining 2.5cm (1in) above the raw top edge of the main fabric (in other words, in line with the top edge of the buckram), slipstitch (see page 17) the folded side edges of the lining to the folded side edges of the main curtain.

6 Fold and press a 2cm (¾in) turning along the lower edge of the main curtain fabric, then turn up the remaining 8cm (3¼in) of the hem allowance and slipstitch in place, to lie 1.5cm (½in) beneath the lining.

7 With the pelmet and main curtain laid out flat, pin, baste, and machine stitch along the folded top edge of the lining, stitching along the top edge of the concealed buckram. Fold the pelmet over to the right side of the curtain along this line.

8 For each tie, lay two strips of fabric with right sides together and stitch down one long side, across one end, and up the other long side, taking 12mm (½in) seam allowances. Trim across the corners; turn the strip right side out, and press. Fold in the seam allowances at the remaining short end, and slipstitch.

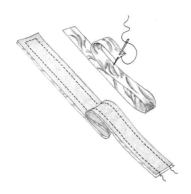

9 Spacing the ties at regular intervals, fold each tie in half to find the centre, and firmly stitch the centre of each tie to the top edge of the curtain.

This tonal architectural print subtly introduces pattern into a very plain room. The single curtain at this tall, narrow window has a short self-pelmet (integral valance) as well as a tie-on heading. The black wrought-iron curtain pole accentuates the contemporary mood of the room.

FABRIC-COVERED BOXES

For a stylish solution to bedroom clutter, cover a set of boxes with fabric. The boxes should be reasonably rigid and sturdy – ordinary shoe boxes might be a bit flimsy, but office box files or storage boxes made of heavy cardboard are ideal. The boxes that photocopy paper comes in are also useful, as they are sturdy and are a versatile size and shape. Similarly, fabric that has some body and thickness and does not fray easily will give the best result. Cover all your boxes to match, coordinate, or tie in with a single theme. We have chosen checks, but you could go for flowers, paisley motifs, or, in a child's room, characters from nursery rhymes, or favourite stories. If you decide on a set of boxes that are identical to start with, different covers will allow you to identify their contents.

A selection of containers in lots of different sizes and shapes is useful and looks very stylish: tiny ones for earrings or pins, medium-sized ones for gloves, belts, and scarves or letters and photographs, and extra-large ones for spare bedlinen and out-of-season clothing.

All over the house, extra storage in this neat, portable form can prove extremely useful – in the bathroom for soaps, in the kitchen for clipped-out recipes, in a sewing corner as a charming alternative to a sewing basket, in a working conservatory for seed packets and catalogues, or in a study for stationery.

YOU WILL NEED

CARDBOARD BOX, WITH LID
MEDIUM-WEIGHT FABRIC
LIGHTWEIGHT FABRIC, FOR LINING
(OPTIONAL)
ROLLER BLIND (ROLLER SHADE) STIFFENER
(OPTIONAL)
CLEAR-DRYING PVA (WHITE) GLUE
BRASS LABEL PLATE, WITH ATTACHING
SCREWS

Make sure the scale of the pattern you choose for your fabric-covered boxes suits their dimensions; for each one in our coordinated set, we've used cotton check of a different size. If you are covering many boxes, add in a patterned fabric or a stripe to make the collection more interesting.

1 Measure and cut fabric pieces for the box as follows: for each end, cut fabric to the exact dimensions, plus a 12mm (½in) allowance on each of the four edges; for each long side, cut fabric to the exact measurement, plus a 12mm (½in) allowance at the top and bottom only; for the base, cut a piece to the exact measurement. For the lid, measure the dimensions of the lid top and the depth of the sides, then cut a single piece that is as long as the length of the lid plus four side depths, and as wide as the width of the lid plus four side depths.

2 If you are lining the box, cut a piece to the base measurement, plus two side depths, less 6mm (¼in) each way. From each corner remove a square the size of the depth measurement, less 3mm (⅛in). Also cut a piece to the size of the lid top.

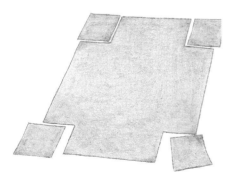

3 To help prevent the raw edges from fraying, you can, if you wish, spray them with roller blind (roller shade) stiffener before covering the box.

4 To cover the ends of the box, first cut a 12mm (½in) square from all four corners of each of the two fabric end pieces. Using clear-drying PVA (white) glue, glue a fabric end piece to each end of the box, placing it centrally. Stick down the overlaps at the sides, then glue the top overlap to the inside and the bottom overlap to the base.

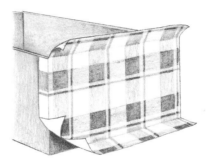

5 Next, glue a fabric side piece to each of the two sides, placing it centrally and gluing the top overlap to the inside and the bottom one to the base. Cover the underneath of the box with the fabric base piece. Use extra fabric glue at the raw edges to prevent fraying.

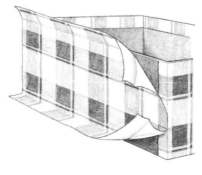

6 If you are lining the box, insert the lining, bringing the overlaps up the sides and making sure that they meet neatly at the inside corners.

7 From the piece cut for the lid, cut out and remove a square measuring twice the lid depth measurement from each of the four corners. Glue the fabric to the lid, placing it centrally and sticking the overlapping edges onto the inside. If you are adding a lining, glue the lining piece to the inside top of the lid.

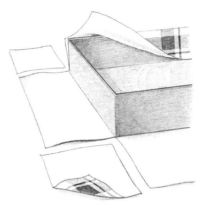

8 Attach the brass plate to one end of the box and add the label.

FABRIC-COVERED SCREENS

Another time-honoured furnishing piece designed to protect against draughts and provide privacy is a hinged screen. Historically, tall ones – sometimes with as many as eight or even twelve panels – were called draught screens (although the very large ones were really portable partitions), and the lower ones were known as chair screens. They both fulfilled largely the same functions, however, and, like bed curtains, added a strong decorative touch in their own right, since they were often covered with intricate embroidery or tapestry.

In a modern bedroom, an attractive screen could prove invaluable for concealing a plain but useful piece of storage furniture, a dressing corner, or a washbasin. If your window and its view are lovely to look at, eschew curtains or blinds altogether and simply move a screen in front of it at bedtime. A screen can also look decorative placed between a bed and the wall instead of a bedhead. Or, elsewhere in the house, use a screen to define activity areas within a large room, such as a dining area or home-office corner in a large living room.

There are two basic types of screen that are fairly easy to make yourself. One type is constructed of lightweight flat panels covered with fabric and hinged together, which give a simple, tailored look. The other consists of hinged wooden frames onto which widths of fabric are gathered; these look softer and less formal. In both cases, you might be lucky enough to find old screens that are in good condition and need only recovering.

If you choose a flat screen, stretch your fabric over each panel and either anchor it along the edges with decorative tacks or, as we have done, use a staple gun, covering the staples later with ribbon, braid, gimp, or wooden beading. To give a padded look, attach a layer of synthetic wadding (batting) to both sides of each panel before you fix the cover in place.

The advantage of a gathered-fabric screen is that you can remove the cover fairly easily for washing, or when you want to replace it. This type looks equally effective in a light, flimsy material such as lace or muslin, or in a traditional furnishing fabric such as chintz. If you want your screen to look the same from both sides, use two pieces of material placed wrong sides together for each panel.

Fitting furniture glides on the bottom edges will make the screen easy to move around, an important factor on heavy screens in particular.

We've edged our screen with simple beige gimp to focus attention on the pretty checked fabric. For an alternative look, cover the panels with plain fabric and choose a contrasting shade or multi-coloured design for the edging.

PANEL SCREEN

YOU WILL NEED

3 PRE-CUT PANELS MDF (MEDIUM-DENSITY
FIBREBOARD), E1 THICKNESS, OR 2.5CM (1IN)
THICK (PARTICLE BOARD IN THE US)
FABRIC
STAPLE GUN AND UPHOLSTERY STAPLES
GIMP OR OTHER BRAID, 2.5CM (1IN) WIDE
PVA GLUE AND 2.5CM (1IN) PAINTBRUSH
6 TWO-WAY SCREEN HINGES
6 FURNITURE GLIDES

MEASURING

The three fibreboard panels should be wide enough in relation to the height to maintain stability but not so large that the screen is too heavy. The panels of the screen featured here are 160cm (64in) high and 55cm (21½in) wide, which is the maximum size that would be practicable with MDF of this thickness. You will need sufficient fabric to cover the back and front of each panel, plus a 12mm (½in) turning at each edge, and enough gimp to run around each panel.

1 Buy the MDF panels pre-cut to the correct size. For each panel, cut two fabric pieces, each with a 12mm (½in) turning all around. (Or cut one piece for each panel with a 12mm (½in) seam allowance all around; it will be folded in half.)

2 Lay an MDF panel face up on a flat surface and staple one fabric piece to the edges of the fibreboard. Begin with staples at the centre top and bottom, and then put staples at the centre point at each side, making sure that the fabric is pulled taut and even. Return to the top and bottom, and work out gradually to the corners. When you have finished stapling along the top

and bottom, repeat the process at the sides, again working outwards to the corners. Make neat folds at the corners.

3 Turn the panel over, and cover the back in the same way. To cover the staples, glue gimp or other braid around the edge, brushing the glue onto both the fabric and the wrong side of the edging and smoothing it along the edge of the panel. Start and finish with straight cut edges, meeting at a point about 13cm (5in) in from the corner, on the bottom edge.

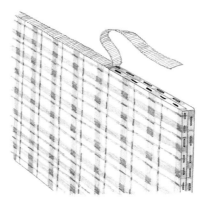

4 Make two more panels in the same way, and then leave all three panels to dry, lying flat.

5 Attach three pairs of hinges to adjacent panels, setting one hinge approximately 13cm (5in) down from the top, another the same distance up from the bottom edge and a third in the middle, and attaching the corresponding hinge of each pair on the adjacent panel. Repeat for the other three pairs of hinges. Hammer furniture glides to the bottom edges, two for each panel, setting them 12.5cm (5in) in from the corners so that the edging join will be covered and protected.

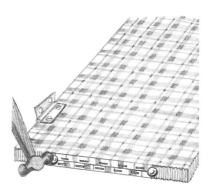

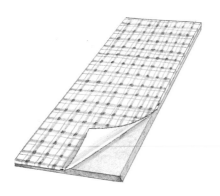

GATHERED SCREEN

YOU WILL NEED

3 WOODEN FRAMES OF THE DESIRED SIZE

12 RING SCREWS AND 6 LENGTHS OF CURTAIN
WIRE, TO BE STRETCHED BETWEEN SCREWS
INSIDE THE FRAME

2 COORDINATING FABRICS, OF THE SAME
WEIGHT AND TYPE

6 TWO-WAY SCREEN HINGES

6 FURNITURE GLIDES

MEASURING

When you have chosen the frames, measure the inner edge, from top to bottom and from side to side; for each panel you will need a piece of each fabric as long as the length measurement of the panel plus 8.5cm (3½in), and as wide as twice the width measurement of the panel since each panel is gathered.

1 Fix four ring screws to the inside of each frame, positioning them 2.5cm (1in) down from the top and the same space up from the bottom inner edge.

2 Lay coordinating fabric pieces, with right sides together, and pin, tack (baste), and stitch the side seams, stopping 9cm (3¾in) short of the raw edge at the top and bottom.

3 Turn the fabric right side out. Turn in and press the unstitched part of the side turnings at the top and bottom. Also turn in and press a 5cm (2in) allowance along the top and bottom edges; catch-stitch in place.

4 For the casing at the top edge, make three lines of stitching: one close to the foldline; one 2.5cm (1in) from the foldline, and one 3.7cm (1½in) from the foldline. Repeat for the casing at the bottom edge.

5 Thread curtain wire through the lower channel of the top casing and the upper channel of the bottom casing, gathering the fabric onto the wires. Attach the fabric panel to the rings. Repeat for the remaining panels, then add hinges and glides, as for the fabric-covered screen.

81

PADDED HANGERS WITH SACHETS

To pamper your clothes and add a delightful, fragrant detail to the inside of your wardrobe or cupboard at the same time, make up a set of padded, fabric-covered hangers with a scented sachet – matching or otherwise – hung on each one. These padded hangers would also make very special gifts, or ideal novelties to sell at school or church sales.

Padded hangers are simply ordinary wooden hangers wound round with strips of synthetic wadding (batting), then covered with a sleeve of fabric. Make your sachets in the form of tiny drawstring bags, or cut them out in circle, square, or heart shapes. Choose a fairly

lightweight material in a plain colour or a suitably small print, and leave both hanger and sachet plain; or trim them with lace, ribbon, or broderie anglaise (eyelet).

When they are finished, fill your sachets with lavender or dried herbs, and hang them from a length of lace or satin ribbon or a strip of matching fabric. Alternatively, make up several scented bags separately, and tuck them among folded items of clothing or between the sheets and pillowcases in your linen drawer. If your fabric is not tightly woven enough to hold dried lavender, make a small inner sack out of muslin to put inside the sachet.

YOU WILL NEED

FOR THE HANGER:
PLAIN WOODEN COAT HANGER
MEDIUM WEIGHT POLYESTER WADDING
COVERING FABRIC
MATCHING SEWING THREAD

FOR THE SCENTED SACHET:
FINE, CLOSELY WOVEN FABRIC
MATCHING SEWING THREAD
RIBBON FOR THE TIE
DRIED LAVENDER OR POT POURRI
SPRIG OF DRIED LAVENDER (OPTIONAL)

Add finishing touches to the decorating scheme with items like our padded hanger, which was covered to coordinate with the other accessories in the room. As an alternative, use fabric remnants or scraps left over from a sewing project. A small amount of extra material would make a matching sachet – we've chosen fine muslin for ours.

Hanger

1 First wind a strip of wadding, approximately 10 x 90cm (4 x 36in), around the wooden part of the coat hanger, from end to end. Make sure that the ends are well padded, and manipulate the wadding into a good shape. (You may need to make a few holding stitches to secure the wadding, or simply tie it on with thread.)

2 Cut a strip of fabric 15cm (6in) deep and the length of the wood plus 10cm (4in). Fold the fabric in half lengthwise, and trim each short end into a semicircle – use a glass to draw the shape first.

3 With the fabric folded lengthwise, and with right sides facing, stitch the shaped ends of the hanger, taking 12mm (½in) seam allowances.

4 Turn the fabric right side out, then fold in and press a 12mm (½in) seam allowance down each long raw edge. Place the fabric over the hanger; bring the pressed edges together along the top of the hanger, gathering them to fit, and neatly sew, using either a running stitch or slipstitch (see pages 24 and 18 respectively) depending on the effect you want.

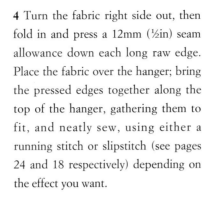

Scented sachet

1 Cut a piece of fabric that measures 10 x 33cm (4 x 13in).

2 Fold the fabric in half crosswise, with right sides together, and stitch down each long side, taking a 12mm (½in) seam allowance. Neaten the raw edges.

3 Make a double 6mm (¼in) turning around the top edge of the sachet and slipstitch in place.

4 Cut a length of ribbon measuring approximately 75cm (30in), so that it will be long enough to tie the scented sachet to the hanger and make a bow at the top.

5 Cut a second length, approximately 50cm (20in), to tie around the sachet.

6 Stitch the centre of the shorter ribbon to the centre of the back of the bag, approximately 5cm (2in) down from the top edge.

7 Fold the longer ribbon in half, and place the folded end over the stitched portion of the first ribbon, at right angles to it and with the tails running upwards. Stitch it to the ribbon and back of the bag.

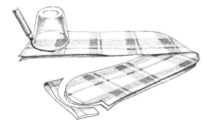

8 Half-fill the bag with lavender or pot pourri and tie the underneath ribbon into a bow at the front.

9 Use the top ribbon to tie the bag to the padded hanger (or any ordinary hanger), making a bow at the front and tucking a sprig of dried lavender into the bow if desired.

TRIMMING BEDLINEN

To give a lovely finish to your bedlinen, add your own edging. On classic white cotton or linen, you could stitch a length of trimming, either narrow or wide, such as cotton lace, ribbon, or broderie anglaise (eyelet) along one edge of each top sheet, and perhaps along the hem of each pillowcase as well. Or, for a subtler effect, set the trimming a little way in from the edge as we have done; this option might be a better choice for a duvet cover, whose thickness could overwhelm a dainty border trim. Wide lace or ribbon should be hand sewn along both edges, or machine sewn using a zig-zag stitch. Narrow trimming can be anchored with a single row of stitches down the centre.

It's important that any edging you use is capable of withstanding repeated washing and ironing at fairly high temperatures; if in doubt, test a short length of the edging before you begin. Whatever trimming you choose, however, it's a good idea to pre-wash it before you sew it on in case it shrinks slightly.

BUTTONED CUSHION COVER

Another quick, stylish cushion cover that is very easy to make is one that takes the form of an envelope. Suitable for any straight-sided cushion pad, this cover can be sewn from a single piece of fabric the same width as the pad, plus seam allowances, and about 2½ times its length. Simply fold this long rectangle with right sides together to make a pocket the same size as the pad, and stitch the side edges. Turn right side out. Hem the remaining raw edges to make a flap, then fasten this flap down. We fastened it with a row of horn buttons, but ties or hidden press studs (snaps) could be used instead. As an alternative to a straight flap, cut one in a triangular or curved shape, and fasten it with a single novelty button, tie, or toggle.

This envelope construction is the same one used for old-fashioned pyjama or nightdress cases, and these will make instant cushion covers. Look in junk shops and antique markets for lovely old embroidered or linen cases, then just tuck in an appropriately sized pad. Slip-stitch the opening loosely or use poppers (snaps), press studs, or Velcro, so that you can remove the pad when the cover needs washing.

In our restrained, contemporary scheme, we've fastened the cushion covers with large mother-of-pearl buttons, but more intricate or unusual ones could be a decorative feature in their own right. This would be an ideal use for exquisite antique buttons when there aren't enough for the front of a dress or jacket.

INSTANT CURTAINS

To curtain a window without sewing a stitch, start with pairs of appropriately sized squares or rectangles of fabric whose edges are already finished. Sheets (like the monogrammed French linen ones we've used), tablecloths, and lace panels are all suitable, and even large shawls or scarves would suit a small window. Then simply attach them to your pole with the special brass clips intended for display curtains, called curtain clips. (Although these clips come in various sizes, they are not meant to hold a lot of weight so this treatment would not suit very large windows, or very heavy material.)

DISPLAYING TEXTILES

While you're hunting in antique stalls and markets, see if you can find some pieces of old lace like collars and cuffs – either sold separately, or attached to items of clothing that are too worn to serve any useful purpose. Carefully wash and iron the lace, then have it mounted and framed (or do this yourself) and hang it like a conventional picture. Even just lengths of beautiful lace (or ribbon) can look beguiling arranged simply in rows.

To emphasize its intricate patterns, set your lace against a background that affords a subtle contrast. A piece of velvet looks good, and the pile will help to keep the lace in position. Wallpaper or fabric with a tiny, subtle print is also suitable; choose a pattern that features elsewhere in the room, or use a small square of paper or fabric on its own.

If you're lucky enough to possess, or find, wonderful old clothes that are perhaps too frail or impractical to be worn, you could display them on the wall instead of framed pictures. Hang a silk bedjacket or kimono from a length of wooden dowelling slipped through the sleeves, or fold an embroidered shawl over dowelling to make a triangular tapestry. Skilfully arranged on the wall, a collection of ornately beaded evening bags or chic period hats would make a similarly striking display.

Use brass curtain clips to transform an antique linen sheet into a curtain with a deep, self-pelmet (integral valance).

These exquisite antique collars were originally unearthed in a junk-shop.

In our kitchen, we turned homely linen tea towels into cushions and curtains (see pages 53–4 and 58–9), but they can be adapted equally well for use in other rooms. Here, a generously sized tea towel is draped over a wicker storage basket serving as a night table. If you find this look appealing, sew lots of striped or checked linen tea towels together to create a giant bedspread with its own valance made from matching towels stitched end to end. On this bed, a collection of red-and-white gingham fabrics has the same fresh, crisp look, which is made feminine by the frilled white linen.

ABOVE A riot of Regency stripes dominates this totally tented bedroom that would not have looked out of place in the Napoleonic campaigns. The hammock beds and their canopies are hung from supports in the form of crossed spears so that, like all the chairs and stools, they can fold away flat in authentic style – ready, in theory, to move on to the next battle.

OPPOSITE If bare white walls make you want to cover them immediately, hang up a row of tartan blankets. Here, four different tartans, traditionally fringed and folded over to make self-pelmets, blend with those on the table to transform a small, plain room into a plaid paradise. The bold statement of the tartan is balanced by the colonial wooden furniture.

CHAPTER SIX

Children's Rooms

As well as offering a suitable place to play, the ideal children's room should excite and inspire a vivid young imagination, and, in addition, provide secure, comfortable surroundings that are conducive to relaxation, reading, and a peaceful night's sleep. Every furnishing element should be easy to clean, hardwearing, and absolutely safe in every way. Happily, there is an enormous choice of specially designed fabrics and furnishings available that meet all these requirements, and make it easy for you to create the nursery of your child's dreams.

A few generations ago, this wouldn't have been possible. Not until the late Victorian and early Edwardian periods – what many people think of as the heyday of the nursery – did fabrics and wallpapers appear that were designed to suit the needs and interests of the young. Until fairly recently, too, children's rooms were usually furnished with cast-offs from the rest of the house: lumpy chairs, scratched tables, and threadbare rugs that were past the stage when additional damage could do them any harm.

These days, however, modern technology and design have provided materials that not only look sensational, but also withstand

The tented bed in our children's room suits the circus theme perfectly, but, like all the other elements, it can easily adapt to other fantasies, from a princess's castle to an Apache wigwam or a space station. It is even appropriate in an adult room, perhaps, in an antique *toile de Jouy* fabric.

the kind of punishment that only energetic youngsters can inflict. We've used a selection of these to establish a delightful circus theme for a young child's room. Centred around a wonderful tent bed, this theme is reinforced with novelty cushions, a jumbo ball bean-bag, a capacious toy bag, and a range of bedlinen in bright patterns and stripes that suit the mood perfectly.

If your offspring is not inspired by dreams of the big top, choose a different theme – a farmyard perhaps, filled with cows, pigs, ducks, and sheep in the form of stuffed toys and painted decorations as well as printed fabrics and bedlinen. Or pick out one type of creature that your child particularly loves – say, frogs – to base your scheme around, and have fun searching for them in unusual forms such as puppets, bath sponges, and wooden carvings. Another idea is to take inspiration from a well-loved book or film, picking out favourite characters to be featured prominently.

SAFETY CHECKLIST
❏ Ensure all toys and decorations comply with the Toy Safety Standard, which includes using non-toxic paints and smooth wooden finishes. In the United States, check that they comply with, or exceed, US government safety regulations.
❏ Choose fire-retardant materials.
❏ Make sure that every fabric and surface is washable, and that all covers can be removed for laundering.
❏ Avoid any trimmings that could present a choking hazard.
❏ Anchor all buttons, pompons, and other trimmings securely so that there is no danger of tiny fingers working them loose. Small children tend to put everything in their mouths, and a little ball of yarn would be easy to swallow or choke on.
❏ Ensure that curtain tie-backs or cords, hooks, bedposts, etc are fixed out of reach of small children.
❏ A child should not have either a pillow or a duvet before the age of one year.
❏ Make sure that all potential hiding places, such as toy boxes, are well ventilated and that the child cannot be trapped inside.

TENTED BED

Re-create the magical world of the big top in your child's room by turning the bed into a circus tent. The same shape and construction could easily be adapted to make a princess's castle, a play house, a space station, or even an Apache wigwam. For a slightly different effect, remove the pompons and replace the zig-zag edge with scallops – or leave a plain hem which, at some future date, can be decorated with a more grown-up trim of plain or tasselled fringe or some other edging.

The tent's frame is constructed from thick wooden battens, securely screwed together and fixed into the bed base. This wooden structure must be carefully and securely made and is a job for a professional carpenter or a highly skilled amateur. Tracks are fixed to the inside of the timber frame, and the canopy fits over the outside. The cover and curtains are sewn

separately, then slipped into place so that they can be removed for cleaning.

If your child's room is fairly small, you could create a similar effect by constructing a tented ceiling consisting of gathered fabric caught into a central rosette fixed to the ceiling.

Either choose a coordinating paint, paint effect, or wallpaper, or go all the whole way and hang the walls with matching fabric (stretched flat or gathered). To conceal the join between ceiling and walls, fix a short valance with a plain or shaped edge. As for the bed hangings, go for reasonably neutral fabric so that it doesn't have to be replaced every time the room's furnishings undergo a change.

This tented effect is not, of course, suitable only for a nursery; it could look splendid in an adult's bedroom, a dining room, a small entrance hall, or even a bathroom.

YOU WILL NEED

5 x 2.5CM (2 X 1IN), 10 X 2.5 CM (4 X 1IN).
AND 7.5 X 7.5CM (3 X 3IN) TIMBER

WOOD SCREWS

WOOD GLUE

L-BRACKETS (OPTIONAL)

CURTAIN TRACK AND HOOKS

MAIN/OUTER CURTAIN FABRIC

LINING FABRIC – THE SAME WEIGHT AND
TYPE AS THE MAIN FABRIC, BUT IN A
CONTRAST COLOUR

MATCHING SEWING THREAD

COLOURED YARNS FOR POMPONS

CARDBOARD FOR POMPONS

STANDARD HEADING TAPE AND HOOKS

MEASURING

The framework

Use 7.5 x 7.5cm (3 x 3in) timber for the posts; 10 x 2.5cm (4 x 1in) for the pelmet rails, and 5 x 2.5cm (2 x 1in) for the canopy frame and cross supports. The height of the posts and pitch of the roof should be in proportion to the height of the room; for a room with a ceiling 2.6 – 2.7m (8½ – 9ft) high, the posts will be about 1.9m (6ft 4in) high, and the distance from the point of the canopy to the bottom edge of the pelmet rail will be about 75cm (2ft 6in).

The length of the pelmet frame should be the length of the bed plus two thicknesses of pelmet timber and two post thicknesses; for example 195+2.5+2.5+7.5+7.5 = 215cm (78+1+1+3+3 = 86in). The width should be the width of the bed plus two pelmet timber thicknesses: for example, on a single bed, 90+ 2.5+2.5 = 95cm (36+1+1 = 38in).

Two triangular timber frames are required for the canopy; each is made with one (base) piece the same length as the long pelmet rail and two pieces to meet at the peak of the canopy. The distance from the peak to the centre of the long side should be approximately two-thirds the width of the bed.

To give added strength to the structure, cut two cross supports from 5 x 2.5cm (2 x 1in) timber, to the width of the bed.

The canopy

First decide the proportions and height of the tent. When you have made the frame and have fixed the curtain tracks in position, measure from the peak down to the point at which the canopy frame meets each post (a); from the peak down to the centre at one side (b); and from the peak down to the centre of the end above the foot of the bed (c). Also measure the length (d) and the width (e).

Using these measurements, draw triangles on the fabric. It may be advisable to make the canopy a couple of millimetres (⅛ in) too big so it rests gently over the frame and does not have to be stretched.   Add 12mm (½in) to

the sloping sides, and along the lower edge add a band 35cm (14in) deep for a pelmet. Cut two side pieces from main fabric and two from lining fabric, and cut two end pieces from main fabric and two from lining fabric.

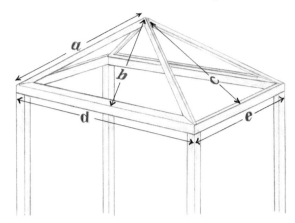

The curtains

Measure from the track down to floor level; all curtains are cut to this length plus 5.5cm (2⅛in). For each of the eight curtains (one at each side of a post) you will need one width of main fabric and the same amount of lining fabric (for a single bed).

ASSEMBLING THE FRAMEWORK

1 First make the pelmet frame, with the 10cm (4in) edge on the vertical, and mitring the corners. Fix the cross supports inside the frame 45cm (18in) in from the head and foot.

2 Next assemble the two triangles for the canopy. The long, lower edge of each triangle is bevelled to sit flat on the top edge of the pelmet frame, as are the edges where the triangles meet.

3 A simple way to join the two triangles together at the apex is by sinking two bolts, one at each side and just below the joint, through both triangles.

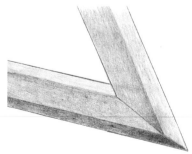

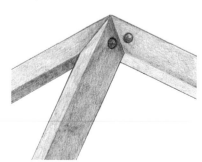

4 Fix the posts into the corners of the pelmet frame, gluing and screwing with the frame flat on the floor and the posts upright, then invert the structure, placing it over the bed. Secure the posts to the bed frame with screws of an appropriate length (such as size 10). If the posts cannot be fixed

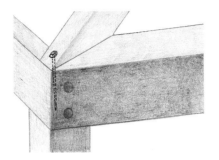

securely to the bed, fix them to the floor with L-brackets.

5 Sit the canopy frame on the pelmet frame and glue and screw it in place. Fix a 40cm (16in) length of curtain track inside the pelmet frame on each side of every corner.

THE CANOPY

1 First, taking 12mm (½in) seam allowances and with right sides together, stitch the four sections of main fabric cut for the canopy together at the side (canopy top) seams, leaving the centre of one of the seams open for 30cm (12in). Try the canopy on the frame now to check it fits. Repeat the process to join the four lining sections in the same way.

2 On the wrong side of the fabric, mark the zig-zag edging along the lower, straight edge of the main fabric with a sharp, hard-lead pencil. Space the triangles evenly, with a half-triangle on each side of a corner so that the zig-zags continue unbroken all the way around the canopy. Our triangles are

approximately 15cm (6in) across at the top, and 17.5cm (7in) from the centre top to the pointed tip.

3 Place the main fabric and lining with right sides together and lower edges matching. Pin and stitch along the marked zig-zag edge, then cut along the edge, trimming almost up to the seamline at the outward points and taking notches out of the seam allowance at inward facing angles.

4 Turn the canopy right side out, bringing it through the open seam in the lining, then slipstitch (see page 17) the seam to close it. Press the seams, especially the zig-zags. Place the canopy over the frame.

CURTAINS

1 For each bed curtain, place the main fabric and the corresponding lining section together with right sides facing and raw edges even. Starting at the top edge, stitch down one side, along the bottom edge and up the other side, taking a 1.5cm (⅝in) seam allowance.

Trim off all corners. Turn the curtains right side out and press them flat.

2 Along the top edge, fold the raw edges to the right side of the curtain (the right side being the fabric that will show on the outside of the bed),

making a 4cm (1½in) turning. Pin the heading tape in position on the right side, setting it 2.5cm (1in) below the folded edge. Stitch it in place, stitching along the top and bottom edges of the tape and down the sides. Insert hooks and hang from the tracks.

POMPONS

Soft woolly pompons like the ones on our tented bed add a delightful touch anywhere in a child's room – lined up along a curtain pelmet, adorning novelty cushions in the form of eyes and nose on a cartoon face or buttons on a Santa Claus jacket, or just colourful, tactile decorations in their own right. You could incorporate miniature pompons in delightful home-made greetings cards and add a touch of fantasy to wrapped presents.

Pompons are easy to make and would make a perfect rainy-day project for older children. In addition, they are an excellent way of using up odd balls of left-over wool.

1 From thin cardboard, cut two circles, each 6.5cm (2½in) in diameter. Cut a 12mm (½in) hole from the centre of each. With the cardboard circles held together, wind yarn through the hole and around the edge. Continue until the hole is completely filled.

2 Cut through the yarn all around the outer edge, then ease the cardboard circles slightly apart and, using strong thread, tie the yarn tightly together at the centre. Wind the thread several times around the centre, and leave the ends to sew the pompon in place.

3 Remove the cardboard circles, cutting them away if necessary, and fluff out the pompon. You may need to trim the ends to make them even. If you are making them for the canopy, make a pompon for each triangle of the zig-zag edging.

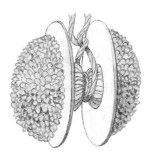
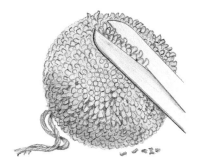

We needed huge, multi-coloured pompons that would add solid colour to our tented bed so we chose wool to make fluffier pompons and picked out colours that toned with the scheme.

BEAN-BAG CUSHION

A large, squashy bean-bag cushion is one of the most versatile items of nursery furniture you can provide. Filled with polystyrene granules, it can be a giant toy as well as a comfy and safe chair for toddlers and young children. Later, with a change of cover, it will provide valuable extra seating for teenage get-togethers. A round bean bag is particularly adaptable; we've made it into a circus ball to tie in with the room's decorating theme, but with the addition of some creative embroidery or appliqué, it could be a giant soccer ball or baseball, a man-in-the-moon, a huge apple, or even a world globe.

Whatever design you choose for your cover, you'll want it to be removable for washing, so it's important to enclose the polystyrene granules in a plain inner lining first. When you make the outer cover, leave one long seam open through which you can insert the inner bag, then slip-stitch the seam closed. A zip fastening would make the outer cover easier to remove, but the only type strong enough would be metal, which might scratch a child. Also, it is relatively difficult to insert a zip into a curved seam. Use fire-retardant material for the outer covering, or a barrier interlining for the inner cover.

YOU WILL NEED

PAPER, FOR PATTERN (WALL LINING PAPER WOULD BE IDEAL)
FIRM PLAIN COTTON, FOR THE INNER COVER
FIRMLY WOVEN COLOURED COTTONS, FOR THE OUTER COVER
MATCHING SEWING THREAD
POLYSTYRENE GRANULES

MAKING THE PATTERN

You will require two pattern pieces – a base and a petal shape. For the base draw a circle 46cm (18in) in diameter, then around it draw a second one 12mm (½in) bigger all around, for the seam allowance. If you cannot find anything of that size to use as a template, tie a pencil to a length of string and use this as a compass. For the smaller circle, the length of the string should be 23cm (9in), and for the larger one 23.5cm (9¼in).

The sides of the bag are formed by eight petal shapes, extending up from the base to meet at the top. The bottom of the petal is one-eighth of the circumference of the smaller circle, in other words 18cm (7in). The petal extends to a height of 62.5cm (25in) at the top point, and is 7.5cm (3in) wider in the centre than at the base.

To make sure that the petal sides are the same, fold your piece of paper lengthwise and draw one half of the petal shape only, drawing the side and half the base. Add a 12mm (½in) seam allowance around the drawn lines, and then cut out and unfold the paper.

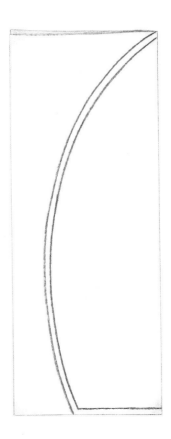

1 Using the pattern pieces, cut one base and eight petals from inner lining fabric, and the same from the outer fabric. (The bean bag seen here has four yellow petals, two green ones, a red, and a blue.)

2 First make the inner cover: join the petals into four pairs, stitching along the long curved edge of each pair. Take a 12mm (½in) seam allowance and, for the point at the top, finish on the seamline, not at the raw edge.

3 Join one pair to another pair. Repeat for two more pairs then join these, leaving a 25cm (10in) gap in one seam. All eight petals should now be joined together. Join the base to the petals, taking a 12mm (½in) seam allowance.

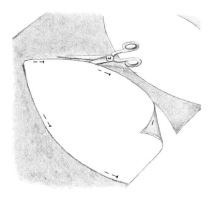

4 Turn the inner bag right side out; fill it with polystyrene granules, then slipstitch the opening (see page 17). Make the outer bag in the same manner, alternating colours. This time, leave an opening of approximately 56cm (22in) in one side. Ease the bean bag into the cover, and finally slipstitch the opening.

LEFT Although polystyrene granules have long since replaced the bean-bag's eponymous original filling, this adaptable and practical item of children's furniture has remained consistently popular for decades.

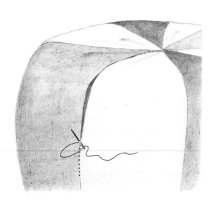

NOVELTY CUSHIONS

Displayed individually as soft pictures, or piled in an inviting heap on the bed or the floor, novelty cushions can be as simple or as intricate as you choose to make them. Try creating a whimsical image of your child, your house, a family pet, or a favourite cartoon character; or use cut-out letters to spell a special name or a message. Make a pretty sky scene on a blue cushion – light blue for day, perhaps, with a bright yellow sun and multi-hued rainbow, and dark blue for night, with a crescent-shaped moon and a scattering of stars. Or compose an underground seascape with fish, shells, and seaweed on a turquoise background.

We've used non-toxic glue to stick felt shapes onto a plain fabric panel in a multi-print cushion cover, but neither the glue nor the felt is washable, so designs made in this way are suited more for decoration than rough-and-tumble. To make safe, washable cushions, cut your shapes out of cotton, then appliqué them into place. To appliqué, set your sewing machine to a close zig-zag stitch, cut each shape to the exact size, tack (baste) it in position, then stitch around the edge. For a satin-stitch effect, run around the shapes a second time.

Another no-sew alternative is to draw or stencil your chosen designs onto plain fabrics with non-toxic fabric paints, pens, or crayons. Fabric crayons are particularly easy to use and are ideal for children who want to decorate their cushions with their own designs.

Our jolly clown is made entirely of felt glued onto a cotton cushion cover. For a more three-dimensional effect, appliqué each piece in place, tucking a layer of synthetic wadding (batting) under the body, then use woolly pompons (see page 96) for his nose and his buttons.

REEFED CURTAIN

Inspired by a style popular in eighteenth-century France, a reefed curtain is almost a cross between a curtain and a blind (shade). Gathered onto a pole, it doesn't draw in the usual way, but pulls up to one corner by means of a cord threaded through rings stitched on the back. This cord is then anchored in place around a cleat fixed to the wall nearby.

Reefed curtains were originally hung in pairs, although today the term is commonly used to describe a curtain used singly. Reefing is also sometimes known as Italian stringing. As well as giving a stylish, asymmetrical effect, this style copes brilliantly with windows that are situated awkwardly – in a corner, perhaps, where there is no room for fabric to stack back on one side, or on a stairwell, where one curtain would drag on the ground. As a striking treatment for a pair of windows, try hanging reefed curtains that pull to both sides, like theatre curtains.

When you want a formal or traditional look, go for a pencil- or pinch-pleat heading and a plain or fringed edge, or a fabric border. For our circus-themed child's room, however, we've chosen a simple gathered heading, and a zig-zag edge that echoes the one on the matching tent bed. The yellow striped lining fabric is also used for the inner lining of the tent bed, further linking the two features.

Make sure when you fix the anchoring cleat (awning cleat) that the cleat and the cord are well out of a child's reach.

We painted our wooden curtain pole and brackets blue and added multi-coloured spots and stripes to reinforce the novelty theme of the room.

YOU WILL NEED

MAIN CURTAIN FABRIC

MATCHING SEWING THREAD

CONTRAST FABRIC OF THE SAME WEIGHT AND
TYPE, FOR THE LINING

STANDARD HEADING TAPE (2-CORD
SHIRRING TAPE)

CARDBOARD

MASKING TAPE

PLASTIC OR BRASS CURTAIN RINGS

THIN NYLON CORD

RING SCREW

CLEAT

MEASURING

The curtain width should be at least 2 to 2½ times the length of the curtain track or pole. This total fabric width is also the measurement for the heading tape required. If you need to join fabric widths, remember to allow extra for seams.

The curtain should be cut to a length of the desired finished length plus 5.5cm (2⅛in). For the total amount of fabric that you will need, multiply this amount by the number of fabric widths required; you will need this quantity of the main fabric and also of the lining fabric.

1 First work out how deep you want to cut your zig-zag edging. This will depend on your fabric, on the height of your windows, and on your own personal preference. The triangles that form the zig-zag edge of our curtain have equal sides, and measure approximately 10cm (4in) from point to base. The simplest method for working out how many zig-zag triangles you can neatly fit into the finished length is actually to draw the complete zig-zag edge to scale on graph paper.

2 When you have decided on the depth of the zig-zags, make a template by drawing a triangle to the full size on graph paper. Cut out the paper shape, glue to cardboard and, using a craft knife, cut out the triangle.

3 On the wrong side of the main curtain fabric, mark off the beginning and end of the zig-zags along the side edge. They start 1.5cm (⅝in) up from the bottom raw edge and finish 4cm (1½in) down from the top raw edge. Using the template and a sharp coloured pencil, mark the zig-zag shapes down the edge of the curtain. The outer points should be set 1.5cm (⅝in) in from the raw edge. The marked line is the stitching line.

4 Lay the main fabric on top of the lining fabric, with right sides together and raw edges even. Pin down the straight edge, across the bottom, and along the zig-zag edge.

5 Machine stitch a 1.5cm (⅝in) seam down the straight edge, across the bottom edge and along the zig-zags, with a machine setting of about 5 stitches to 2.5cm (1in).

6 Cut out the zig-zag edge 12mm (½in) beyond the stitching. Trim across the points, almost up to the stitching line, and take notches out of the inner corners, again almost to the line.

7 Turn right side out, pushing out the points, and press all seams.

8 Along the top edge, fold the raw edges of both layers to the back of the curtain, making a 4cm (1½in) turning. Pin the heading tape in position, setting it 2.5cm (1in) below the folded edge, and turning under the ends of the tape. Stitch it in place, stitching along the top and bottom edges of the tape and down the sides (taking care not to stitch the drawing cords).

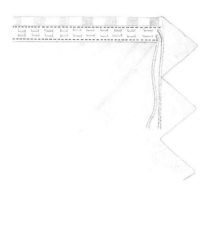

9 Starting from the top of the zig-zag edge, measure down for the length of the curtain track plus an additional 20cm (8in), or to the desired shape of the draped effect. Lay the curtain, backing side upwards, on a flat surface. Mark off points at 20cm (8in) intervals in a straight line leading from the marked point on the zig-zag edge to the opposite top corner of the curtain, immediately below the heading tape. An easy way to do this is to lay a strip of masking tape across the fabric and mark the tape.

10 Sew on a curtain ring at every marked point, finishing with one close to the heading tape, then remove the masking tape. Tie the nylon cord firmly to the ring at the zig-zag edge and thread it through the remaining rings, up to the top corner.

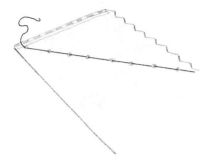

11 Hang the curtain, then fix the ring screw into the window frame, at a point close to the ring stitched to the corner of the curtain. Fix the cleat at a convenient point below the ring screw and bring the cord through the ring screw and around the cleat.

TOY BAG

A big, bright bag with a personalized design can swallow up a great deal of nursery clutter. Run one up in upholstery fabric, canvas, or ticking, and decorate it with appliqué letters or shapes (see page 99) or spell out your child's name with ric-rac or washable ribbon. (If the bag is for a young child, it would be safer to use elastic rather than a drawstring; insert the elastic into the casing, and stitch the opening closed. Hang it from a small fabric loop.)

You could even provide a set of coordinating bags: one for soft toys, one for building blocks, one for puzzles and small games, one for sports equipment, and one for gloves and scarves.

This form of storage can prove extremely useful all over the house. In an adult's bedroom, drawstring bags are ideal for accessories such as socks, belts, scarves, and gloves, or smaller bags for cotton balls or handkerchiefs. In the bathroom, you could have a large bag for laundry, and a smaller one for extra soap.

Hang your personalized drawstring bag from a strip of matching fabric, or thread a length of rope through the casing (see page 115 for making instructions).

To pull a small, awkwardly shaped space together visually, use the same pattern on all its main surfaces. This attic nursery uses a fresh floral stripe on the walls, at the window, and draped from the coronet above the bed. The same material has even been used to re-line the Victorian pram.

A simple timber frame and a pair of
lace-edged gingham curtains have
transformed this recess under the
eaves into a cosy retreat for a young
girl. In the absence of a bedside table, a
narrow shelf has been installed at
mattress height to hold reading
material and bedtime paraphernalia.

CHAPTER SEVEN

Bathrooms

Special rooms for washing were not a common feature of even the grandest houses until the first half of the nineteenth century, and it was only at the end of that century, or even later in some places, that they were installed in ordinary homes. For decades, bathrooms tended to be cold and were endured for as brief a time as possible, but in recent years they have been transformed by advances in heating and plumbing into havens of efficiency and comfort. Invest a little extra time and a touch of flair and you can go even further by creating a room in which long baths and daily ablutions become luxurious, soothing experiences.

Because bathrooms are occupied for relatively short periods, the decorating scheme here can incorporate bright or deep colours or whimsical themes that would quickly pall elsewhere. Remember to choose shades that you can face first thing in the morning and at the end of a long day. If you are doing up your bathroom from scratch, plain white fittings will allow maximum flexibility in selecting design and colour schemes – both initially, and when you fancy a change. Any textiles you choose for this room should be washable and fairly lightweight so they don't absorb and hold damp. This is especially

We've reinforced our seaside look with pieces of driftwood, giant sponges, seaweed-like greenery, and timber accessories left unfinished to suggest the bleached effect of sun and surf. It's worth taking the trouble to colour-coordinate small items such as toothbrushes, soaps, and towels as well.

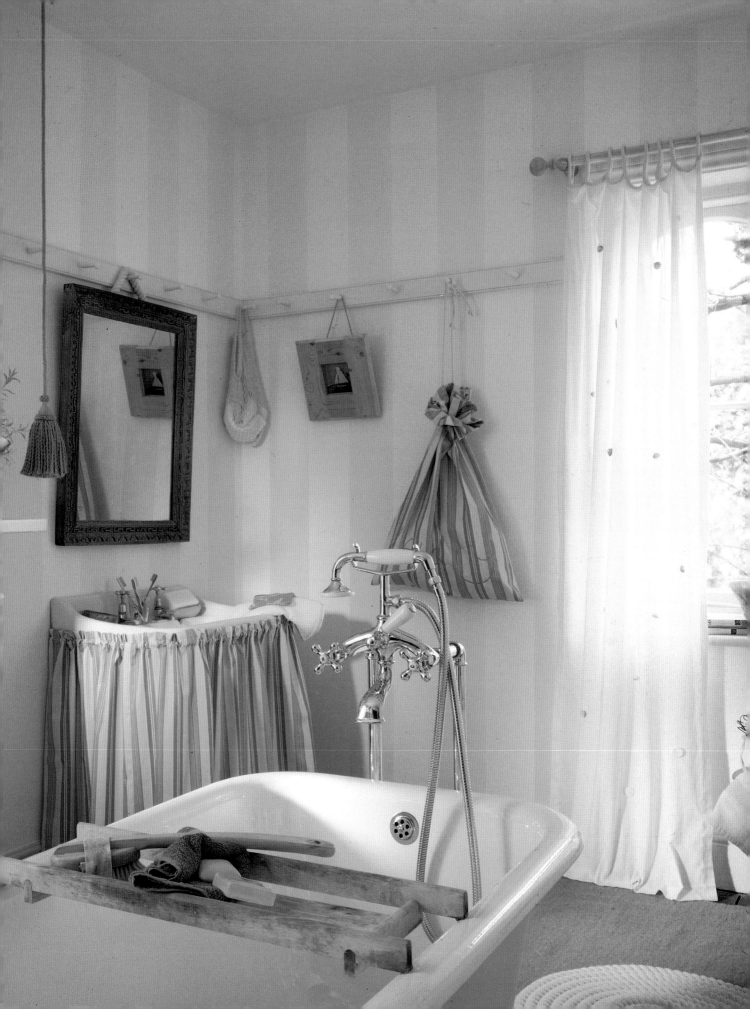

Originally an aid to tidiness in Shaker rooms, peg rails adapt readily for use in the bedroom, the kitchen, and the hall as well as the bathroom.

true in small spaces, where steam and condensation can be a recurring problem.

Here, we've chosen an extremely popular and appropriate decorating theme – the seaside. Like many bathrooms in older houses, this one is quite big because it was converted from a former bedroom. A seaside theme, though, suits rooms of any proportion. We've established the mood by painting the walls in wide cabana stripes, but a watery colourwash might be a better choice in a smaller room. The laundry bag and the skirt on the washbasin are made from strong cotton that is also striped, this time in narrow, deckchair fashion, while the window is hung with diaphanous muslin scattered with seashells. On the floor, plain painted boards are covered with cotton rugs in a pale sea blue that coordinates with the paintwork, and a coil of thick nautical rope ensures that bathers disembark onto a soft, safe surface. To help keep the room shipshape, a practical peg rail copes with hanging storage.

If you are adept with a paintbrush, you could create an alternative sea scene by covering the walls with a freehand mural that depicts an underwater world of tropical fish, coral, and seaweed. Those who are happier with a land-based theme can find inspiration in a wide variety of sources. Try a rich and exotic Indian look using warm reds and saffron yellows; colourwash the walls and print on them with a decorative stamp reminiscent of a wood block print. Alternatively, for a more traditional English look, hand paint wild roses and meadow flowers along the skirting board and hang a pretty floral chintz fabric at the window.

COILED ROPE BATHMAT

As part of our bathroom's nautical theme, this thick cotton bathmat is made from marine rope and is surprisingly soft underfoot. It is coiled into a round shape (you could make an oval one just as easily), and sewn together by hand. For added firmness, glue it to a canvas backing using waterproof adhesive. Available from ship's chandlers in several colours as well as white, this rope has a slight tendency to shrink, so you should wash the bathmat carefully in cool water, using a gentle soap or detergent intended for use with wool. In our bathroom, we've used this chunky rope for hanging the mirror as well. Elsewhere it would make excellent curtain tiebacks or a stitched-on border for a cushion.

This project was inspired by traditional braided rugs, which make charming, country-style accessories for any room. They are hand made from strips of fabric stitched end to end, folded into a tube to conceal the raw edges, then plaited, coiled into a round or oval shape, and sewn or laced together.

YOU WILL NEED

COTTON ROPE, 2.5CM (1IN) IN DIAMETER

WHITE BUTTON THREAD OR OTHER STRONG SEWING THREAD

DARNING NEEDLE

PVA (WHITE)GLUE

WHITE CANVAS – EITHER ARTIST'S CANVAS OR A WIDE DECKCHAIR FABRIC (OPTIONAL)

1 Working on a clear, flat surface, start coiling the rope. Either coil from the centre, to produce a circular rug like that in the picture, or, for an oval shape, start with a straight length (the length will determine the proportions of the finished rug) and form coils around this. As you go, slipstitch (see page 17) the coils firmly together, using a darning needle and strong thread.

2 When you have finished, taper the rope end and brush it with a little PVA glue, to prevent it from unravelling. Tuck it underneath the previous coil and slipstitch in place.

3 The coiled mat can be left as it is, or a canvas backing may be added. Cut canvas to the size of the finished mat, plus a 12mm (½in) turning all around. Turn under the allowance and, making sure that the backing is just a fraction smaller than the mat, sew the backing firmly to the underside of the mat, oversewing (overcasting) through the foldline of the canvas.

A coil of nautical rope stitched together makes a shipshape bathmat.

SHELL CURTAIN

Few people can resist collecting shells at the seaside, and a bathroom scheme based on a marine theme provides a perfect opportunity to put them to good use. Drill tiny holes in a collection of small shells, and sew them onto simple curtains. These can be made from muslin, like ours (but because this material has a tendency to shrink, you should buy at least 10 per cent too much, then pre-wash and iron it before making your curtains) or an open-weave net to suggest fishing nets. Whatever material you choose, be careful only to use only small shells and avoid sewing on too many, since their weight would pull the fabric out of shape.

This idea is suitable not only for full-length curtains, but also for short, or even café curtains. We've hung ours from big open loops made of white cotton nautical rope but simple tabs or standard heading tape would work just as well.

This is a project that children, with supervision, might love to join in. They can collect the shells from a holiday beach and then, when you've drilled the holes, they can help to position the shells before you sew them in place. If shells don't suit your scheme, buttons, ribbon bows, mattress tufts, miniature tassels, or even tiny bells could be used to decorate plain curtains in a similar way.

When your shell curtains need washing, just rinse them through in cool, soapy water and then lay them out flat to dry.

YOU WILL NEED

FIRM, FINELY WOVEN WHITE COTTON FABRIC SUCH AS CASEMENT FABRIC OR MUSLIN

WHITE SEWING THREAD

COTTON ROPE, 12MM (½IN) IN DIAMETER

ABOUT 50 SMALL SHELLS

DARNING NEEDLE

WHITE QUILTING THREAD

BRADAWL (AWL) OR FINE DRILL

The charm of these shell-scattered curtains lies in their simplicity. Shells stitched onto muslin make a charming window treatment that filters light and provides privacy. The original rope heading accentuates the nautical twist.

MEASURING

For the width of each curtain, you will need between 2 and 2½ times the length of the pole, divided by two because there are two curtains, plus an allowance of 4cm (1½in) for each side hem.

For the length of each curtain, you will require the finished length (measuring from the point at which the rope loops meet the curtain, down to floor level – or slightly longer if you want the curtain to trail on the floor), plus a total allowance of 10cm (4in) for top and bottom turnings.

The rope must be long enough to run along the full width of the curtain, plus an allowance for each loop. The size of the loops will depend partly on the thickness of your pole; also, loops can be made slightly longer than on our curtains, if this would suit your window frame. The loops were stitched at intervals of approximately 12.5cm (5in), but you may need to adjust this distance slightly so that the loops can be spaced evenly.

1 Wash the shells very thoroughly and allow them to dry, then make a hole in each, using a bradawl (awl) or a fine drill. The curtains seen here used approximately 20 shells for each curtain, but you may break a few when you make the holes.

2 For each curtain, join widths, if necessary, to make the full width, taking 2.5cm (1in) seams. On each side edge, make a double hem by turning in 2cm (¾in) and then the same again, and machine stitch close to the fold. At the top edge, make a double 1cm (⅜in) turning and machine stitch.

3 Using a darning needle and quilting thread, sew the rope in position along the top in the following way. At one side, make the first loop then check that it is big enough for the pole. Sew the loop in place, securing it firmly at the base, then lay the rope along the top of the curtain and stitch the rope to the folded edge of the fabric, taking small travelling stitches and alternating between the fabric and the rope. After about 12.5cm (5in), form a second loop and attach this securely in the same way, then continue sewing the rope to the top edge.

4 Carry on in this way until you reach the opposite edge, and then sew on the final loop, cutting away any extra rope, and ensuring that the end will lie at the back of the curtain, out of sight.

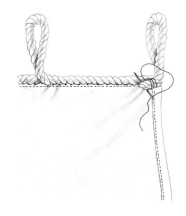

5 At the bottom edge, make a double 4cm (1½in) turning and either hem by hand or machine stitch. (There is no need to mitre the corners of light-weight curtains like this, since the fabric will not be bulky.)

6 Arrange the shells in a random pattern over each curtain. Using an ordinary needle and either sewing thread or quilting thread, sew the shells one by one to the curtain, tying the thread ends in a neat reef knot (square knot – right over left, then left over right) at the back.

SKIRT FOR PEDESTAL BASIN

To give a traditional, "dressed" look to a standard pedestal basin, sew a simple skirt for it in crisp washable cotton. As well as adding a decorative element to your bathroom, a skirt like this provides a useful concealed storage area.

We've chosen a cheerful striped material to reinforce our seaside scheme, but for a more feminine look, use a floral print or even an old-fashioned piece of linen edged in lace, crochet, or embroidery. The skirt has been gathered onto flexible curtain wire threaded through a narrow casing stitched on the back. Alternatively, you could thread it through a simple top hem, but this would not give you the pretty frilled effect illustrated. The ends of this wire, into which screw eyes are inserted, are placed onto wall-fixed hooks. If your basin is flat and straight around the sides, the tension of the wire should keep the skirt securely in place. If the sides are curved or angled, however, you may need to anchor the fabric at several points around the top by means of double-sided adhesive pads, which should peel off fairly easily when you want to remove the skirt for washing.

If your bathroom scheme is masculine and tailored, fit a simple pleated or straight skirt rather than a gathered one. Attach it with a long strip of Velcro, with one side glued around the basin using waterproof PVA (white) glue, and the other stitched to the inside top of the skirt.

YOU WILL NEED

CURTAIN FABRIC

MATCHING SEWING THREAD

FLEXIBLE CURTAIN WIRE AND FIXINGS

MEASURING

To find the length of the fabric, measure from the desired top of the skirt – which will be approximately 4cm (1½in) above the level of the curtain wire – down to the bottom, and add 15cm (6in) for hems. The width of fabric you will need is between 2 and 2½ times the length of the curtain wire. If possible, use whole widths of fabric rather than half-widths to minimize the number of seams. Multiply the number of fabric widths by the length (including hems) to find the amount of fabric required.

1 First attach the curtain wire. The hooks holding the wire for the skirt shown here are firmly attached to the wall at each side, so that the wire can be drawn taut around the basin, holding the skirt in position without any further supports. It might be necessary to have a wooden frame as an additional support, however.

2 Join the fabric widths required to make the total skirt width. At the side edges, make double hems by turning under 12mm (½in) and then turning under the same amount again; machine stitch, close to the foldline.

3 Along the top edge, turn the fabric under by 2.5cm (1in) and press. Turn it under again, this time by 6.5cm (2½in), and press.

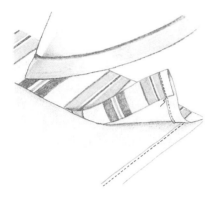

4 Stitch along the folded edge, about 3mm (⅛in) from the foldline. Stitch a second line, 12mm (½in) from the first, to make a casing for the wire.

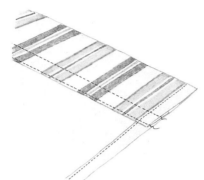

5 At the bottom edge, fold under 12mm (½in), and then 5cm (2in) and hem. Thread the wire through the casing, and attach it to the wall hooks.

TASSEL PULLS

In many bathrooms, either the main light or the one over the basin is controlled by a pull cord rather than a conventional switch. To provide a touch of whimsy, replace the cord with a tasselled rope. One end of a tassel tie-back would be ideal.

If you have an old-fashioned high cistern, replace the chain with a similar bit of trimming – or just tie a tassel on the end. These days tassels are made in a wide range of tempting materials. Look for one in bright cotton, string, raffia, or even paper that ties in with your colour scheme – or choose a neutral one in natural jute.

Use a full-sized tassel to switch on a ceiling light, and a scaled-down version for a wall light with a pull cord.

LAUNDRY BAG

A large drawstring bag can serve a multitude of purposes. Here, it is used for laundry; on page 102, the same bag has become a hold-all for a child's toys. You can also make the bag on a smaller scale, for shoes or to protect handbags. Appliqué a name on the bag, or identify its purpose with machine embroidery as in the photograph.

YOU WILL NEED

FABRIC

MATCHING SEWING THREAD

CORD OR RIBBON, FOR TIES

1 First cut two pieces of fabric, measuring 50 x 90cm (20 x 36in) for the front and back of the bag.

2 If you are labelling the bag, either embroider the name or purpose of the bag, by hand or machine, or cut out letters from a contrast fabric and appliqué them to the bag. For the latter, baste the letters in position on the bag and then stitch around the outside edge of each letter with a close zig-zag stitch or satin stitch.

3 Take the two pieces of main fabric and make a French seam: with wrong sides together and taking a 6mm (¼in) seam allowance, stitch from the top left-hand corner of the bag down to the bottom left-hand corner, along the lower edge, and up the right-hand side, stopping 17.5cm (7in) short of the top right-hand corner.

4 Turn the bag wrong side out and press the seam, then stitch again along the same edges, this time taking a 9mm (⅜in) seam allowance and enclosing the raw edges within the stitching. Again, stop 17.5cm (7in) short of the top corner on the same side.

5 Clip into each seam allowance for 6mm (¼in), at the point where the stitching of the French seam finishes. Starting 4.5cm (1¾in) down from the top raw edge of the bag, stitch the side seam for 10cm (4in), taking a 1.5cm (⅝in) seam allowance.

6 Starting where the French seam stops, neaten both sides of the seam allowance up to the top. To do this, turn each raw edge under for 6mm (¼in) and then for another 9mm (⅜in) and slipstitch (see page 17) in place.

7 At the top edge, turn 6mm (¼in) to the wrong side, and press. Now turn 8.5cm (3⅜in) to the wrong side.

8 Stitch around the top of the bag, 8.2cm (3¼in) down from the top edge. Now stitch around the top of the bag again, this time 5cm (2in) down from the top edge of the bag, making a channel for the tie. Turn right side out.

9 Thread the cord or ribbon through the channel. You can either knot the ends of the tie together, or overlap them and sew them together so that they are permanently tied.

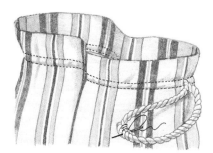

LINED BASKETS

Store small bottles, tubes, bars of soap, facecloths, and jars safely and close to hand in a pretty basket made from wire or wicker. To keep your baskets clean and prevent small items from falling through, make a lining for each one from practical towelling (terrycloth), as we have done, or choose a printed cotton that you've used elsewhere in the room. Just cut a piece of fabric to the required shape and bind the edges with bias binding (see page 23, step 6 for how to do this), leaving loose ends that can anchor your lining in place. When it gets dirty, a quick machine wash will make it look like new. These baskets can be used for storage all over the house.

We've chosen a wire basket to hold our bathroom bits and pieces, but a traditional wicker one might be more suitable for another scheme. If you are lining a wicker basket that is tightly woven, thread the bias binding through a darning needle so that you can tie the cover in place.

OPPOSITE Setting the basin into a vanity unit provides useful counter space, and allows you to choose the height you find most comfortable. The storage shelves underneath this white surface have been concealed behind a pleated skirt in fresh blue checks.

ABOVE This opulent scheme, full of gilded accessories and rococo details owes more than a little to eighteenth-century France. The English chintz makes the scheme less serious and more romantic.

RIGHT Only odd flashes of white porcelain, enamel, and marble reveal the utilitarian function of this luxurious room. The fringed paisley festoon blind (balloon shade), the formal coronet-topped drape over the bath, the plump cushions, and the padded ottoman and stool would all be perfectly at home in a Victorian drawing room.

CHAPTER EIGHT

Garden Rooms

Commonly believed to be a Victorian invention, the conservatory actually became popular a century earlier, with the elegant Georgian orangerie in which exotic fruits were grown. The heyday of the conservatory was, however, in the Victorian era, when, as well as serving as an additional sitting room, it was used for growing ferns and other exotic plants brought back from the distant outposts of the British Empire. Whereas the Georgian orangerie was in the style of the rest of the house, with a slate or tiled roof, the Victorian conservatory was constructed of glass and iron, most often painted green. In the Edwardian era, conservatories became less ornate.

Whether they're elaborate glass-and-iron structures or simple brick extensions, conservatories have a way of providing a seductive link between inside and out that often makes them the most popular room in the house. Even if you aren't able to cultivate exotic tropical trees, flowers, and fruit the way the Victorians did, you can still enjoy being surrounded by streaming sunlight, a profusion of climbing plants, and colourful blooms tumbling out of pots and troughs. Used in clever, creative ways, textiles can add even more to the charm of a garden room by enhancing its visual appeal and making it relaxing and comfortable at the same time.

In common with the flowering plants crowded onto every surface, the natural fabrics chosen for this inviting conservatory have a fresh, outdoor look that belies their considerable strength. Simple stripes and coordinating tonal leaf patterns woven in tender creams and greens blend unobtrusively with the greenery and allow the flowers to dominate.

Unfortunately, the sunshine that you and your plants love so much can do considerable damage to fabrics; few dyes are so stable that they can survive constant exposure to direct light without fading, but some fabrics, usually those of higher quality, are more resistant to fading than others. Deep, rich colours, especially deep blue, are particularly affected by fading in sunlight. We solved this problem by covering the most exposed area – the windows – with natural undyed cotton. If you decide on a plain colour or a print, make sure your chosen design is reasonably colourfast, then line any curtains or blinds for extra protection. It's a good idea to look for fade-resistant fabric for other soft furnishings as well, although few surfaces are as vulnerable to the sun's rays as window dressings. Even if your curtains and chair covers do eventually fade a little, you may find that you have grown to appreciate their gentle, time-worn look.

Direct exposure to sunlight can also weaken fibres, so don't be disappointed if the fabrics in your garden room wear more quickly than those elsewhere in the home. Another consideration is damp, especially in a working conservatory where it's vital to maintain a high level of humidity, so stick to lightweight materials that are easy to wash and quick to dry.

In our long, tiled room, we've chosen a subtle green-and-cream colour scheme that looks enchanting yet keeps the visual focus firmly where it belongs – on the geraniums and the greenery. As an alternative, you could reinforce the riot of blooms with an assortment of coordinating flowery prints at the windows and on the chairs, or keep it simple with an array of plain hues – perhaps bright Provençal colours like yellow, indigo, and scarlet, or more muted shades like burgundy, jade, and smoke. To create an old-fashioned Edwardian look, use canvas and strong cotton in low-key stripes and classic conservatory colours such as dark green.

GARDEN CANE CURTAIN POLE

If the curtains or blinds in your conservatory are fairly lightweight, reinforce the herbaceous theme by replacing standard curtain tracks or poles with lengths of ordinary garden cane intended for staking sweet peas and runner beans. This is available in an assortment of different lengths, and it's also fairly easy to cut with a small hacksaw to give a perfect fit. A very natural material, cane blends perfectly with the other surfaces usually found in conservatories, such as brick, stone, wood, and terracotta.

To use garden cane as a curtain pole, hang it between large brass cup hooks instead of the heavy, purpose-made brackets, used for conventional curtain poles and, where necessary, use small curtain rings, which are also made from brass, to hang the curtains from the ceiling.

Of course, you could copy this idea in any room that has a fresh, uncontrived look; hang café curtains in the kitchen from a short length of cane, or combine the cane with filmy muslin drapes in the bedroom.

ROLL-UP BLIND

One of the nicest, and the simplest, blinds (shades) imaginable is a flat rectangle of fabric that ties onto a pole at the top, and rolls up from the bottom; two lengths of tape hold it in place at the required height.

Our garden room is not overlooked, so the blinds extend only a short way down the window to block out glare. If you will want yours to stay in a rolled-up position much further down, make sure your tapes are long enough to reach that far. Also, because longer blinds are heavier, the tapes should be anchored, for extra strength, around the pole at the top, rather than just around the fabric as we have done.

The uncomplicated construction of these blinds means that they have to be operated by hand. This isn't a problem in many conservatories and garden rooms, since the windows are not veiled every evening and uncovered every morning in the same way that they are in other rooms. If you will want to raise and lower your blinds every day, however, you might be better off with a more sophisticated design such as roller or Roman blinds.

We've used lightweight, natural-coloured cotton at our windows, with leaf-green tapes for contrast. The advantage of plain fabric is that it makes an unassuming backdrop for a dramatic display of plants and flowers, and it looks just as nice from the outside as it does from indoors.

If you prefer a pattern, look for a woven check or stripe that is the same on both sides, or line your blind, either with standard curtain lining or with another layer of your chosen fabric. A lining such as this, of course, will make your blind much heavier, so if you're using two layers of heavy cotton, you may need to use a sturdier pole and stronger tape.

YOU WILL NEED

WHITE OR CREAM MEDIUM-WEIGHT
COTTON FABRIC

MATCHING SEWING THREAD

COTTON TAPE, 12MM (½IN) WIDE

COLOURED WEBBING, TAPE, OR GROSGRAIN
RIBBON 5CM (2IN) WIDE

BAMBOO POLE

WOODEN DOWEL, 18MM (¾IN) IN DIAMETER

TWO LARGE SCREW HOOKS, TO HOLD THE
BAMBOO POLE

MEASURING

Measure the desired pole length (here, from inside corner to inside corner of the window frame). Cut a piece of stout bamboo (for the top pole) and also a piece of dowel (for the bottom of the blind) to this length.

Cut medium-weight cotton fabric to this length for the blind itself. The width should be the pole length plus 5cm (2in). For the length, measure from just below the bamboo pole down to the bottom of the window, and add 15cm (6in).

1 Make double 12mm (½in) turnings to the wrong side down each side edge of the blind fabric; press and then machine stitch.

2 Make a double 12mm (½in) turning along the top edge; press and stitch, as for the side edges.

3 Along the bottom edge, make a casing for the dowel: first turn under and stitch a double 12mm (½in) hem, as for the side and top edges; then make another turning, this time 5cm (2in) deep. Stitch along the double hem stitching line, leaving the ends open, so the dowel can be pushed through the casings.

4 Cut cotton tape into 30cm (12in) lengths to make ties. For each tie, fold a length of tape in half, and stitch the doubled centre firmly to the top, hemmed edge of the blind, as shown. Put a tie at each corner, and then at intervals of approximately 15cm (6in) all along the top edge.

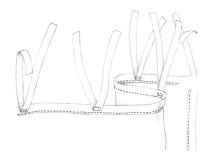

5 Push the dowel through the casing at the bottom of the blind. Screw in the hooks to hold the bamboo and push the pole into position.

6 Tie the blind to the pole, tying the end ties to the ends of the pole that extend beyond the screws.

7 Decide how low you will wish to lower the blind when it is not dropped to its maximum length, and cut lengths of coloured webbing to twice this depth, plus about 45cm (18in) extra, to tie. The webbing lengths are simply wrapped around the blind, at intervals of about 60cm (24in), and tied, as shown in the picture, to hold the blind. If your fabric is heavier, attach the coloured webbing around the bamboo pole at the top as well.

We've used matching ties to fix our blinds onto their pole, but it could also be threaded through a hem or a casing stitched on the back of the fabric. In place of tape, try holding your blind in position with coloured webbing or grosgrain ribbon.

YOU WILL NEED

MAIN CURTAIN FABRIC

MATCHING SEWING THREAD

LINING FABRIC

STRIP OF BUCKRAM, 10CM (4IN) WIDE
(OPTIONAL)

A TOGGLE OR BUTTON FOR EACH TAB

CURTAIN POLE

OPPOSITE Although it's brand new, the charming leaf print used to recover this old and graceful cane chair has a timeless quality that suggests they've always been together.

BELOW At the end of each chevron-tipped tab on our door curtain, we've stitched a wooden toggle for decoration. Large horn buttons would also harmonize with the natural theme.

TAB CURTAIN

Fastened to a pole with simple tabs and toggles, this curtain can also work as a pair of curtains for a window. It looks smart in any room that has an informal feeling, and it is particularly suitable for country-style schemes. It looks just as good short or even café-length as it does full-length. The instructions include stiffening the heading with buckram, but if you prefer a soft look as we did, you could omit the buckram.

MEASURING

First measure the width of the curtain pole and the length of the drop from 5cm (2in) below the pole to floor level. The main curtain fabric should be one-and-a-half times the width of the pole plus an allowance of 8cm (3in) for side turnings, and the length of the drop plus 2.5cm (1in) for the top turning and a further 10cm (4in) for the bottom hem.

The lining fabric should be a width that is one-and-a-half times the width of the pole, and a length that is the length of the drop plus 2.5cm (1in) for the top turning and 6.5cm (2½in) for the bottom hem.

The width of the tabs can be varied to suit your fabric. Ours were each made from two strips of fabric, 7.5cm (3in) wide and 23cm (9in) long, including seam allowances.

You may also wish to use a 10cm (4in) deep band of buckram, to the width of the finished curtain.

1 Lockstitch the strip of buckram (if using) to the back of the fabric (see page 17), leaving a 4cm (1½in) turning allowance at each side edge, and setting the top long edge of the buckram 2.5cm (1in) down from the top raw edge of the curtain fabric.

2 Turn back and press a 4cm (1½in) turning down each side of the curtain and a 2.5cm (1in) turning along the top edge. Turn back and press a 2cm (¾in) turning down each side of the lining and a 2.5cm (1in) turning along the top edge of the lining.

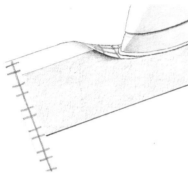

3 Turn, press, and stitch a double 4cm (1½in) hem along the bottom edge of the lining fabric. With the top, folded edge of the lining meeting the top, folded edge of the main fabric, pin the two together along the top and down the side edges.

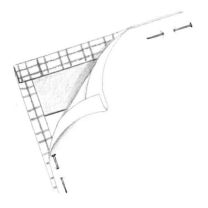

4 Fold and press a 2cm (¾in) turning along the lower edge of the main curtain fabric, then turn up the remaining 8cm (3¼in) and slipstitch (see page 17) in place, to lie below the lining. Slipstitch the lining to the main fabric down the side edges.

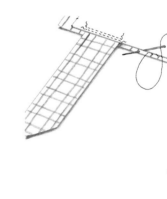

5 For each tab, lay two strips of fabric with right sides together and stitch down two long sides and down to a point at one end, taking 12mm (½in) seam allowances (see page 135, step 4). Trim across the point and corners; turn the strip right side out, and press. At the remaining short end of the tabs, neaten the raw edges together.

6 Spacing the tabs at regular intervals, place the neatened ends of the tabs between the top, folded edges of the curtain lining and main fabric, so that 2.5cm (1in) of each tab is concealed. Pin, baste, and slipstitch the folded top edges together, working a double line of stitches on the tabs themselves to make sure they are firmly stitched into the curtain; the stitches will be concealed by the tabs at the front of the curtain. (Allowing the folded edge of the main fabric to show slightly above the folded edge of the lining when seen from the back will ensure that the lining is not visible from the front of the curtain.)

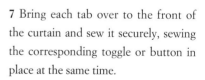

7 Bring each tab over to the front of the curtain and sew it securely, sewing the corresponding toggle or button in place at the same time.

8 Slot the pole through the tabs of the finished curtain.

PADDED LINING FOR WICKER CHAIR

Combine the charming conservatory feel of cane, wicker, rattan, or Lloyd Loom furniture, with the comfort of traditional upholstery by adding a thickly padded lining to a classic woven armchair. The result is so pretty and practical that it would be ideal in a bedroom, a dining room, or a living room, as well as on the lawn at high summer.

The padding comes in two parts: a single shaped section for the back and arms, and a fitted squab cushion for the seat. The squab cushion is made from foam which complies with fire safety regulations. We would suggest a minimum density of 30. If, however, you prefer a feather or polyester cushion, take your template to a professional cushion maker – listed in the telephone directory – and get one made to the correct size.) The shaped section consists of a piece of synthetic wadding (batting) sandwiched between two pieces of fabric. Ours is not attached to the chair permanently, because it needs to be removable for washing, and the main body of our chair is made from a double layer of rattan through which it would be impossible to get anchoring stitches.

If your chair has a thinner construction, a very stylish alternative is to make the lining close-fitting by stitching through the cane or wicker into the piping all around the inside edge; a few buttons across the back and inside the arms will hold it firmly in position and add to the visual interest. Our other padded chair, with its plain, armless shape, was dealt with in a similar way – its padding was already in place, so we just removed the edge strips of cane, replaced the old material with new, and then put back the cane strips, which conceal the raw edges and also the fixings.

For seating of this kind, it is more practical to use upholstery-weight material in a washable fibre such as cotton or linen. We've chosen a subtle jacquard weave with a suitably sylvan motif, but a small, all-over design would also work well. It's a good idea to go for a plain colour or a small or medium-sized pattern, since the effect of a very large one could be lost. Medium-depth colours are best, since dark shades can look too heavy with cane or wicker, and pale colours need washing more often. For your own safety, buy match-resistant fabric.

YOU WILL NEED

PAPER, FOR THE PATTERN (WALL LINING PAPER IS IDEAL)

UPHOLSTERY FABRIC

MATCHING SEWING THREAD

MEDIUM-WEIGHT POLYESTER WADDING (BATTING)

5-8CM (2-3CM) THICK FOAM, FOR SEAT

PRE-SHRUNK PIPING CORD

ZIP, 10CM (4IN) LONGER THAN WIDTH OF BACK (OPTIONAL)

MAKING THE PATTERN

To work out quantities, first make a pattern. Start by making a paper template for the seat – cover the seat with paper and run your finger or folded scissors around the sides, then trim to shape. In the same way, trim and shape a pattern piece to run around the sides and the back, starting and finishing with the front curve of the arms. When calculating fabric quantities, allow for twice the pattern sizes, plus 12mm (½in) seam allowances, a gusset (border) for the seat, and 90cm (36in) extra for piping.

OPPOSITE **A traditional upholstered wing chair shape but made in rattan is very suitable in a conservatory. To ensure a perfect fit for the lining of your wicker chair, make a paper template of its shape from which you can cut both the fabric and the padding.**

Making piping

You will require sufficient piping to run around the upper and lower edges of the seat cushion, and around the top edge of the back and sides padding. The piping cord is covered with bias strips cut from the upholstery fabric.

1 To make the bias binding to cover the cord, find the bias by folding one corner of the fabric so that the selvedge is parallel to the crosswise grain (below left). Press this fold, then mark lines across the fabric parallel to this and 2.5cm (1in) apart using a long ruler (yardstick) and dressmaker's chalk, or a sharp coloured pencil.

2 Cut out the strips and join the ends with right sides together, positioning them so that the raw edges will be in a straight line. Press the stitched seams and trim off the points.

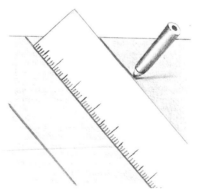

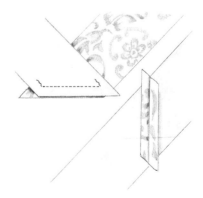

3 To make the piping, place the cord down the centre of the binding, on the wrong side, and fold the binding over the cord. Baste close to the cord, and, using either the zipper foot or the piping foot of your machine, stitch along the basted line.

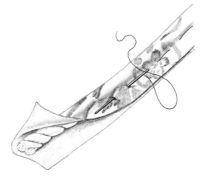
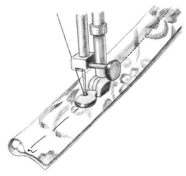

Making the seat cushion

1 First, mark the template shape on foam and cut to shape – a well-sharpened carving knife is easier to use than scissors for this.

2 From fabric, cut two shapes to the size of the template, plus a 12mm (½in) seam allowance all around. Also cut a gusset strip to run all around the seat, cutting it to the depth of the foam plus a 12mm (½in) seam allowance on all sides. If you wish to insert a zip so that the cover can easily be removed for washing, cut the gusset in three sections: one to run across the front and two-thirds of the way down each side, and two pieces to run across the back and one-third of the way round each side. The two pieces should be cut to the length of the back plus two-thirds of a side (plus two seam allowances), and to half the depth of the gusset, plus two seam allowances. Set the zip into the seam which joins these two pieces and then join the gusset into a circle.

3 Lay piping around the seamline, starting at the middle of the back edge, on the right side of the seat top, with seam allowances facing outwards. Pin, baste, and stitch the piping to the seat top, using the zipper foot or piping foot of your machine.

4 At the front corners stitch around in a curved line, and then cut notches from the seam allowance of the cord binding, for a smooth effect so that the piping will lie smoothly and will not cause the fabric to pull at the corners.

5 Where the two ends of piping have to be joined, first unpick the covering for about 2.5cm (1in) and join the bias strips. Unravel the cord ends, trim the strands to different lengths, and then loosely weave them together, to make a smooth join. Finally, fold the binding over the piping cord and complete the piping stitching.

6 In the same way, pin, baste, and stitch piping around the seat bottom.

7 With right sides together, stitch the gusset to the seat top.

8 Still with right sides together, stitch the matching long edge of the gusset to the seat bottom, leaving an opening down one side (or the zip open, if you have inserted a zip).

9 Turn the cover right side out, insert the foam, and slipstitch the opening closed (or close the zip).

Back and sides

1 Using the paper template, cut a piece from wadding (batting), adding a 12mm (½in) seam allowance all around. Cut two pieces to this size from fabric.

2 Prepare covered piping, and with the piping on the right side of the fabric, and seam allowances outwards, stitch piping to one of the fabric sections: up the front edge, along the side, across the back, and then down to the opposite front edge. Use the zipper foot and stitch along the seamline.

3 Baste the wadding to the wrong side of the remaining fabric piece. Lay the two prepared fabric pieces with right sides together and raw edges even, enclosing the piping, and join all along the piped edge. Trim the wadding close to the seamline.

4 On the lower edge, trim the wadding back to the seamline within the seam allowance. Fold the seam allowance of the back fabric section over the backing and turn under the allowance of the front section. Turn the piece right sides out; pin and stitch the lower edge close to the folded edges.

5 To help to hold the wadding in place, and make the back section fit more comfortably, topstitch from top to bottom on each side, at the line where the chair back meets the side.

6 If desired, fabric ties may be added to the top corners of the back section to secure it to the chair. These can be made from left-over strips of the bias-cut fabric, raw edges stitched together, turned inside out, ends neatened, folded lengthwise, and stitched to the back section at the piped seam.

REVAMPING DECK AND DIRECTOR'S CHAIRS

For practicality, value, and style, it's very hard to find anything that rivals classic deck chairs and director's chairs. Made in time-honoured fashion from wood and canvas, they fold away flat for storage, and emerge time and time again to provide instant and comfortable seating in or near the garden.

Give a new look to old chairs in which the frames are still sound by replacing their worn or faded covers with brand-new ones. For a change from the plain and striped canvas sold for the purpose, use upholstery fabric, doubling it for extra strength. To estimate how much you'll need, carefully remove your old covers and use them as a buying and cutting guide; if they've stretched out of shape slightly, take that into consideration. Good-quality fabrics intended for upholstery are strong enough to support a reasonable weight, as long as you use strong thread to sew them – double rows of stitching would be an excellent idea. If you require extra strength, back the upholstery fabric onto standard canvas, perhaps adding an extra detail by slipping in a thin layer of synthetic wadding (batting) and anchoring the layers together with simple lines of quilting.

Remember, though, that while purpose-made canvas will stand up to almost any weather conditions, upholstery fabric is not treated for outdoor use, so keep your chairs out of the rain, and never leave them in the garden overnight, when the morning dew will take its toll. In the same way, if they're not in constant use in a conservatory, store them indoors.

For our folding chairs, we've chosen two fabrics in fresh green: a pale leaf pattern for the director's chair, and a bold stripe for the deck chair and its ingenious matching cushion, which buttons on so it can be removed for washing.

Like our door curtain, this deck chair has functional tab detailing. Here, the buttons are not merely decorative – they hold the head cushion firmly in place and make it easy to remove for washing.

YOU WILL NEED

FOR THE DECK CHAIR:
FIRMLY WOVEN UPHOLSTERY FABRIC
MATCHING SEWING THREAD
DECK CHAIR CANVAS (OPTIONAL)
QUILTING THREAD, OR OTHER STRONG
THREAD
CUSHION PAD
4 BUTTONS
30CM (12IN) ZIP
FURNITURE TACKS
HAMMER

FOR THE DIRECTOR'S CHAIR:
FIRMLY WOVEN UPHOLSTERY FABRIC
MATCHING SEWING THREAD
DECK CHAIR CANVAS (OPTIONAL)
QUILTING THREAD, OR OTHER STRONG
THREAD
FURNITURE TACKS
HAMMER

MEASURING

Deck chair

Start by carefully removing tacks from both ends of the chair, to release the old canvas. Use this as a pattern for the new fabric, but allow an additional 10cm (4in) on the width measurement, for turnings. If you are adding a canvas backing, buy canvas to the same measurements as the old canvas.

For the head rest, you will require a cushion pad the width of the existing chair cover, and approximately 25cm (10in) deep. Cut one piece of upholstery fabric to the measurements of the cushion pad, plus 2.5cm (1in) each way. Cut two more pieces of the fabric to the same length as the first piece, and to half the depth of the cushion pad plus 4cm (1½in). Finally, cut eight pieces, each of them measuring 6.5 x 25cm (2½ x 10in), for tabs.

Director's chair

Remove the old back cover and measure the length of this, excluding any turnings at the ends, and add 5cm (2in) to this. Also measure the depth and add 2.5cm (1in) to that. Cut two pieces of fabric to these measurements.

For the seat cover, start by cutting away the old canvas from each edge rail of the seat, using a sharp knife. Cut the remaining canvas away from around the nails, then carefully hammer these below the surface of the wood. Open out the chair and measure across from the outside edge of one rail to the other outside edge. You will require fabric cut to this measurement plus 5cm (2in) and the depth of the existing cover plus 7.5cm (3in). If you are adding a canvas backing, you will require canvas cut to the same width as the fabric, and to the depth without the extra 7.5cm (3in).

Deck chair

1 If you are backing the cover with canvas, centre the canvas on the wrong side of the fabric. To ensure that the canvas and fabric do not ride apart in use, quilt the canvas unobtrusively to the fabric. The deck chair fabric shown here could be quilted in straight lines from top to bottom, along the outer edges of the wide green bands. Alternatively, in the case of fabric like that used for the director's chair, some of the leaves in the pattern could be outlined.

2 Turn under a double 2.5cm (1in) hem down each long side, enclosing the canvas backing if you are using it. Machine stitch both side hems, using strong thread. For added strength, make a double row of stitching down each of these hems.

3 Along each short edge, turn under and baste a 2.5cm (1in) turning. Lay the fabric, wrong side up, on a flat surface and place the chair frame over it, aligning the long edges. At the top edge, bring the fabric over the bar of the chair and around to the back. Hammer a tack at the centre back, then work outwards to each side, hammering in three more tacks, which are evenly spaced, at each side. Repeat at the bottom bar.

4 To prepare the tabs, place two of the fabric rectangles with right sides together. Taking a 12mm (½in) seam allowance, stitch down one long side, stopping 4cm (1½in) short of the end and angling in to make a point at the centre of one short edge; continue in this way to the opposite long edge and

stitch down that edge. Trim excess fabric from the pointed edge, trimming almost up to the seamline across the point. Turn right side out.

5 Using the button bar of your sewing machine, or stitching by hand, make a buttonhole in the pointed end of the tab. Prepare the remaining three tabs in the same way.

6 For the cushion pad, join the two smaller pieces along one long edge, with right sides together and taking a 2.5cm (1in) seam allowance Leave a 30cm (12in) gap in the centre, and insert a zip in the gap.

7 With the zip open, place the back and front of the cushion cover with right sides together and stitch around the outer edge, taking a 12mm (½in) seam allowance. Trim across the corners and then turn the cover right side out. Insert the cushion pad, and then close the zip.

8 Bringing the square ends of the tabs around to the back of the bar, and spacing the tabs evenly, hammer in tacks to secure the tabs to the deck chair, as for the main cover (step 3).

9 Hold the cushion in place on the chair, and mark the button positions. Remove the cushion pad and sew on the buttons, then replace the pad and button the cushion head rest in place.

Director's chair

1 For the chair back, stitch the two pieces of fabric together down each long side with right sides facing and taking 12mm (½in) seam allowances.

2 Turn the fabric right side out and press; for added strength, reinforce the

Even when you don't have a garden room or a garden, attractively covered director's chairs make ideal extra seating indoors, since they fold away neatly when not in use.

edges by topstitching down each pressed long edge again, 6mm (¼in) in from the edge.

3 At each short edge, turn both layers of fabric under for 2.5cm (1in) and stitch. Lay one short edge over the wooden upright and, starting from the

centre, hammer tacks through the edge of the fabric into the back of the wood. Repeat on the opposite side.

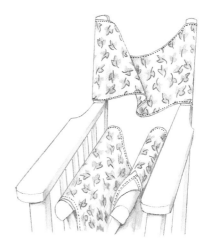

4 For the seat, fold under a double 2.5cm (1in) hem along each long edge and stitch, enclosing the canvas if using (see deck chair, steps 1 and 2).

5 Fold a 2.5cm (1in) turning along each short edge and press. With the chair folded, lay a folded edge along the outer edge of one seat rail and, starting from the centre, hammer tacks through the edge to fix the cover to the rail. Fix the cover to the opposite side rail in the same way.

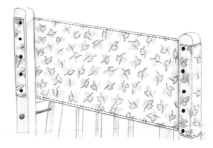

Huge striped awnings have transformed the large open terrace of this urban apartment into a bright and sheltered additional room. In the foreground, the black finish and cover on a contemporary deck chair give it an unexpectedly sophisticated look.

This loggia in Florida has been transformed into an informal family sitting room. The cushions on the rattan peacock chair and two occasional chairs match the loose-covered banquette and the Roman blind (shade).

The long fringed blind set in the open alcove has been made to fit the arch exactly. Hints of pink in the cushions on the banquette match the flowers, while the neutral colour scheme is a cool foil to the lush green garden.

STOCKISTS AND SUPPLIERS

UNITED KINGDOM

The Blue Door
77 Church Road
London SW13 9HH
0181-748 9785

BWS Needlecraft Ltd
1a Tempsford Street
Kempston
Bedford MK42 8HR
Full range of Anchor embroidery threads
01234-841370

Colefax and Fowler
118 Garratt Lane
London SW18 4DJ
0181-874 6484
Chintz fabrics

Christopher Wray's Lighting Emporium
600 Kings Road
London SW6 2YW
0171-736 8434
For lamps, bases, fittings and fixtures

DMC Creative World Ltd
Pullman Road
Wigston
Leicester LE18 2DY
0116-2811040
For pearl and stranded cottons, canvas, linens
and other needlework accessories

George Weil
Showroom
18 Hanson Street
London W1P 7DB
0171-580 3763

Mail order
Reading Arch Road
Redhill
Surrey RH1 1H6
For dyes, fabric paints and fabrics

Hess and Co
7 Warple Mews
Warple Way
London W3 0RS
0181-746 1366
For interlinings and linings

John Lewis Partnership plc
(all branches)
Oxford Street
London W1Z 1EX
0171-629 7711
Excellent haberdashary department

Ian Mankin
109 Regent's Park Road
London NW1 8UR
0171-722 0997

Just Fabrics
Burford Antique Centre
Cheltenham Road
Burford
Oxon OX8 4JA
01993-823391
Plain coloured chintzes and other materials

Liberty
210-220 Regent Street
London W1R 6AH
0171-734 1234
Plain and patterned cotton fabrics, silks and
linens

The Natural Fabric Company
Wessex Place
127 High Street
Hungerford
Berks RG17 0DL
01468-684002

VV Rouleaux
10 Symons Street
Sloane Square
London SW3 2TJ
0171-730 3125
For an exceptional selection of ribbons, braids,
cords, tassels and other trimmings.

Sanderson
112/120 Brompton Road
London SW3 1JJ
0171-584 3344

UNITED STATES

ABC Carpet & Home
888 Broadway
New York
NY 10003
(212) 473-3000

André Bon
979 Third Avenue
New York
NY 10022
(212) 355-4012

Clarence House
979 Third Avenue
New York
NY 10022
(212) 753-2890

Liberty of London
108 West 39th Street
New York
NY 10018
(212) 391-2150

Pierre Deux Fabrics
870 Madison Avenue
New York
NY 10021
(212) 570-9343

Scalamandre
950 Third Avenue
New York
NY 10022
(212) 980-3888

J. Schumacher & Company
79 Madison Avenue
New York
NY 10016
(212) 213-7900

Standard Trimming Co.
306 East 62nd Street
New York, NY 10021
(212) 355-4012

UNITED KINGDOM
LONDON SHOPS
Brent Cross (clothes only) 0181 202 2679
Chelsea 0171 823 7550
Covent Garden 0171 240 1997
Ealing 0181 579 5197
Kensington 0171 938 3751
Knightsbridge (clothes only) 0171 823 9700
Knightsbridge (home furnishings only) 0171 235 9797
Marble Arch 0171 355 1363
Oxford Circus 0171 437 9760

COUNTRY SHOPS
Aberdeen 01224 625787
Aylesbury 01296 84574
Banbury 01295 271295
Barnet 0181 449 9866
Bath 01225 460341
Bedford 01234 211416
Belfast 01232 233313
Beverley 01482 872444
Birmingham 0121 631 2842
Bishops Stortford 01279 655613
Bournemouth (clothes only) 01202 293764
Brighton 01273 205304
Bristol, Broadmead 0117 9221011
Bristol, Clifton 0117 9277468
Bromley 0181 290 6620
Bury St Edmunds 01284 755658
Cambridge 01223 351378
Canterbury 01227 450961
Cardiff 01222 340808
Carlisle 01228 48810
Chelmsford 01245 359602
Cheltenham 01242 580770
Chester (clothes only) 01244 313964
Chester (home furnishings only) 01224 316403
Chichester 01243 775255
Colchester 01206 562692
Derby 01332 361642
Dudley 01384 79730
Eastbourne 01323 411955
Edinburgh (clothes only) 0131 225 1218
Edinburgh (home furnishings only) 0131 225 1121
Epsom 01372 739595
Exeter 01392 53949
Farnham 01252 712812
Gateshead 0191 493 2411
Glasgow 0141 226 5040
Guildford 01483 34152
Harrogate 01423 526799
Heathrow 0181 759 1951
Hereford 01432 272446
High Wycombe 01494 442394
Hitchin 01462 420445
Horsham 01403 259052
Ipswich 01473 216828
Ipswich 01473 721124
Isle of Man 01624 801213
Jersey 01534 608084

Kings Lynn 01553 768881
Kingston 0181 549 0055
Leamington Spa 01926 314584
Leeds 01132 450622
Leicester 01162 513165
Lincoln 01522 511611
Llanidloes 01686 412557
Maidstone 01622 750138
Manchester 0161 834 7335
Middlesbrough 01642 226034
Milton Keynes 01908 660190
Newcastle-Under-Lyme 01782 662014
Newport I.O.W. 01983 821806
Northampton (clothes only) 01604 231975
Norwich 01603 632958
Nottingham 01159 503366
Oxford 01865 791689
Perth 01738 623141
Peterborough 01733 311766
Plymouth 01752 268344
Preston 01772 202425
Reading 01734 594313
Richmond 0181 940 9556
Salisbury 01722 338383
Sheffield 0114 2701855
Sheffield Meadowhall 01742 568221
Shrewsbury 01743 351467
Skipton 01756 700301
Solihull 0121 704 4344
Southampton 01703 228944
Southport 01704 546214
St Albans 01727 864611
Stockport 0161 474 7927
Stratford-Upon-Avon 01789 298852
Sutton 0181 643 9790
Sutton Coldfield 0121 355 3671
Swindon 01793 641727
Taunton 01823 288202
Tenterden 01580 765188
Torquay 01803 291443
Truro 01872 223019
Tunbridge Wells 01892 534431
Watford 01923 254411
Wilmslow 01625 535331
Winchester 01962 855716
Windsor (clothes only) 01753 854345
Windsor (home furnishings only) 01753 831456
Wolverhampton 01902 27293
Worcester 01905 20177
Worthing 01903 205160
Yeovil 01935 79863
York 01904 627707

REPUBLIC OF IRELAND SHOPS
Cork 00 35 32 127 4070
Dublin 00 35 31 679 5433

HOMEBASES
Within Sainsbury's Homebase House and Garden Centres
Basildon 01268 584088
Basingstoke 01256 469510
Bath 01225 339293

Blackheath 0181 856 9767
Bradford 01274 611929
Branksome 01202 768311
Brentford 0181 847 2214
Camberley 01276 686227
Cardiff 01222 499675
Catford 0181 461 0606
Chelmsford 01245 257257
Chichester 01243 533373
Colchester 01206 869187
Coventry 01203 715901
Crawley 01293 538351
Crayford 01322 558614
Croydon 0181 684 8250
Derby 01332 291260
Enfield 0181 366 2236
Gloucester 01452 526806
Guildford 01483 304115
Harlow 01279 413355
Hatfield 01707 275837
Hendon 0181 200 7737
Hull 01482 572434
Ilford 0181 590 0212
Ipswich 01473 721124
Kensington 0171 603 2285
Kingston 0181 949 7861
Leeds 0113 2685010
Leicester 0116 2546075
Luton 0582 593445
Maidstone 01622 715400
Mill Hill 0181 203 7740
Milton Keynes 01908 692727
New Southgate 0181 368 1698
Newcastle-Under-Lyme 01782 711752
Northampton 01604 234143
Norwich 01603 417474
Nottingham 0115 9413885
Oldbury 0121 544 7333
Orpington 01689 890353
Oxford 01865 747979
Penge 0181 778 4214
Rayleigh Weir 01268 745374
Reading 01734 584572
Richmond 0181 876 2235
Rochester 01634 200088
Romford 01708 730326
Sheffield 0174 2555175
Southampton 01703 510098
Stockport 0161 474 7489
Swansea 01792 650935
Swindon 01793 487125
Tunbridge Wells 01892 546646
Wakefield 01924 387011
Walsall 01922 29524
Walsgrave 01203 602086
Waltham Cross 01992 625275
Walthamstow 0181 531 8233
Watford 01923 252075
Willesden 0181 459 3989
Wimbledon 0181 946 9802
Worcester 01905 420401
Worle 01934 512628
York 01904 643911

UNITED STATES OF AMERICA
Albany 518 452 4998

Ann Arbor 313 747 6620
Annapolis 410 268 6906
Ardmore 215 896 8293/0208
Arlington 703 415 2111
Atlanta-Lenox 404 231 0685
Atlanta-Perimeter 404 395 6027
Austin 512 451 4036
Bal Harbour 305 864 5628
Beachwood 216 831 7621
Birch Run 517 624 9297
Birmingham 205 985 0090
Bluffton 803 837 2366
Boca Raton 407 368 5622
Boston 617 536 0505
Bridgewater 908 725 3700
Buffalo 716 681 8600
Burlington/Boston 617 272 4540
Burlington/Vermont 802 658 5006
Cambridge 617 576 3690
Carmel-by-the-Sea 408 624 8095
Central Valley 914 928 4561
Charleston 803 723 3967
Charlotte 704 362 0926
Charlottesville 804 971 7707
Chattanooga 615 855 5496
Chestnut Hill 617 965 7640
Chestnut Hill 215 242 9262
Chicago 312 951 8004
Cincinnati 513 793 5535
Columbus 614 224 5057
Corte Madera 415 924 5770
Costa Mesa 714 545 9322
Cranston 401 946 1211
Dallas-Galleria 214 980 9858
Dallas Northpark 214 369 5755
Danbury 203 790 5068
Dayton 513 299 9007
Denver 303 571 0050
Denver-Cherry Creek 303 322 9401
Des Moines 515 243 8881
Destin 904 654 2626
Edina 612 920 2811
Fairfax 703 352 7960
Farmington 203 521 8967
Fort Lauderdale 305 563 2300
Fort Worth 817 346 4666
Freeport 207 865 3300
Germantown 901 756 7036
Gilroy 408 848 5470
Glendale 818 242 0428
Grand Rapids 616 942 6828
Greenville 302 575 1653
Greenwich 203 661 5678
Grosse Pointe 313 886 6960
Hackensack 201 488 0130
Hingham 617 740 4122
Honolulu 808 942 5200
Houston 713 871 9669
Houston/West Oaks 713 558 6113 +971 9669 +622 2262
Indianapolis 317 848 9855
Jacksonville 904 358 7548
Jeffersonville 614 948 2016
Kansas City 816 931 0731
King of Prussia 610 354 9137
Knoxville 615 558 6385
Lake Forest 708 615 1405

Lancaster 717 397 7116
Lexington 606 253 1724
Little Rock 501 666 0272
Los Angeles 310 854 0490
Los Angeles 310 553 0807
Louisville 502 585 2424
Manhasset 516 365 4636
McLean 703 827 0074
Miami 305 233 8911
Milwaukee 414 347 1930
Minnetonka 612 546 4613
Montgomery 205 284 7011
Myrtle Beach 803 236 4244
Nashville 615 383 0131
New Haven 203 782 9436
New Orleans 504 522 9403
New York City/Westside 212 496 5110
New York City/57th Street 212 752 7300
New York City/South Street Seaport 212 809 3555
Newport 401 846 6980
North Bethesda 301 984 3223
Northbrook 708 480 1660
Novi 313 348 9260
Oakbrook 708 572 9195
Oklahoma City 405 848 6252
Omaha 402 390 2085
Orlando 407 351 2785
Osage Beach 314 348 1337
Owings Mills 410 363 2455
Palm Beach 407 832 3188
Palm Beach Gardens 407 624 5901
Palm Springs 619 322 2099
Palo Alto 415 328 0560
Paramus 201 599 0650
Phoenix 602 956 6043
Pittsburgh 412 367 8881
Pittsburgh 412 621 0735
Pleasanton 510 463 8714
Portland 503 224 0703
Prince William 703 494 3124
Princeton 609 683 4760
Raleigh 919 781 1076
Reading 610 478 9604
Redondo Beach 310 542 4436
Richmond 804 644 1050
Richmond 804 740 1406
Ridgeland 601 957 9063
Rochester 507 287 1073
Sacramento 916 923 5696
Salt Lake City 801 363 8408
San Antonio 210 377 2833
San Diego 619 234 0663
San Diego 619 452 6116
San Francisco 415 788 0190
San Marcos 512 396 5570
Santa Ana 714 834 1211
Santa Barbara 805 682 8878
Santa Clara 408 244 3551
Scarsdale 914 723 8500
Schaumberg 708 619 9110
Seattle 206 343 9637
Secausus 201 863 3066
Short Hills 201 467 5657
Skokie 708 673 6604

Southampton 516 287 2104
Stamford 203 324 1067
Stony Brook 516 689 6622
St Augustine 904 823 9533
St Louis 314 993 4410
Tampa 813 253 2177
Towson 410 825 0362
Troy 810 649 0890
Tulsa 918 749 5001
Walnut Creek 510 947 5920
Washington 202 686 4331
Washington 202 338 5481 +686 1200
Westport 203 226 7495
Williamsburg 804 229 0353
Williamsburg 319 668 1555
Winston Salem 919 760 3733
Winter Park 407 740 8900
Woodbury 516 367 2810
Woodland Hills 818 346 7560
Worthington 614 433 9011

MOTHER AND CHILD SHOPS
Birmingham 205 987 7566
Chestnut Hill 617 965 5687
Cincinnati 513 891 0192
Denver-Cherry Creek 303 322 9403
Farmington-Hartford 203 561 4870
Hackensack-Riverside 201 342 1222
Houston 713 622 2262
Kansas City 816 931 2810
King of Prussia 610 354 9137
New Orleans 504 586 8652
North Bethesda-White Flint 301 230 0081
Princeton 609 683 1300
Redondo Beach 310 542 6228
Schaumberg 708 240 1910
Short Hills 201 467 5657
Stamford 203 359 9902
Tulsa 918 749 5001
Walnut Creek 510 947 3932
Washington 202 686 4333

HOME FURNISHING STORES
Alexandria 701 739 2144
Ardmore 215 896 8293
Atlanta 404 842 0102
Boston 617 357 5151
Burlingame 415 344 1774
Costa Mesa 714 545 7927
Dallas 214 691 6871
Kansas City 816 531 8971
New York City 212 755 5000
Ridgewood 201 670 0868
Short Hills 201 564 9600
Washington 202 686 1200

CANADA
Willowdale 416 223-9507
Calgary, Alberta 403 269-4090
London, Ontario 519 434-1703
Montreal 514 284-9225
Ottawa 613 238-4882
Quebec 418 659-6660
Sherway Gardens, Etobicoke 416 620-7222

Toronto 416 922-7761
Toronto-Yorkdale 416 256-2040
Vancouver 604 688-8729
Winnipeg 204 943-3093

AUSTRALIA
VICTORIA
Armadale 03 509 3365
Camberwell 03 882 3986
Doncaster 03 840 1487
Geelong 05 221 3709
Melbourne 03 602 1268
Melbourne 03 663 7096
Melbourne 03 655 1680
Richmond 03 427 9268
South Melbourne 03 690 9666
South Yarra 03 827 4735

SOUTH AUSTRALIA
Adelaide 08 232 5211

WESTERN AUSTRALIA
Perth 09 321 2391
Karrinyup 09 445 1177

TASMANIA
Hobart Tas 002 34 3484

NEW SOUTH WALES
Sydney 02 261 2458
Sydney 02 232 2829
Chatswood 02 419 5352
Double Bay 02 327 1799
Mosman 02 968 1314
North Ryde 02 805 0665
Kotara 049 56 2836
Chatswood 02 411 9113

ACT
Canberra 06 285-2378
Civic 06 274-3309

QUEENSLAND
Brisbane 07 229-3982

EUROPE
AUSTRIA
Graz 0316 844398/844397
Innsbruck 0512 579254/579257
Linz 070 797700
Salzburg 0662 840344
Vienna 01 5129312

BELGIUM
Antwerp 03 2343461
Brussels (clothes only) 02 5128639
Brussels (home furnishings) 02 5120447
Gent 092 240819

FRANCE
Paris
94 rue de Rennes 1 45 48 43 89
95 avenue Raymond Poincare 1 45 01 24 73
261 rue Saint Honoré 1 42 86 84 13

Galeries Lafayette, 40 boulevard Haussmann (Prêt-à-porter)
1 42 82 34 56, (Décoration) 1 42 82 04 11
Au Printemps
Printemps de la Mode, 64 blvd. Haussmann 1 42 82 52 10
Printemps de la Maison 1 42 82 44 20 (Décoration)
Centre Commercial Parly
Niveau 1, (Décoration), 1 39 54 22 44
Niveau 2, (Prêt-à-porter), 1 39 54 22 44
Centre Commercial Velizy
Niveau 2, (Prêt-à-porter), 1 30 70 87 66
Niveau 3, (Décoration), 1 30 70 87 66
Toulon 94 21 89 58

Aix en Provence 42 27 31 92
Bordeaux 56 44 10 30
Clermont-Ferrand 73 31 22 05
Dijon 80 30 04 44
Gonesse 48 63 25 87
Lille 20 06 90 06
Lyon 78 37 18 19
Nancy 83 35 21 09
Nantes 40 73 17 18
Nice 93 16 06 93
Rouen 35 70 20 02
Strasbourg 88 75 18 90
Toulouse 61 21 38 85

GERMANY
Aachen 0241 30316
Augsburg 0821 154021
Berlin 030 2183016
Berlin (home furnishings only) 030 8826201
Berlin (clothes only) 030 8824934
Bielefeld 0521 177188
Bonn 0228 654908/653930
Bremen 0421 170443
Cologne 0221 2580470
Dortmund 0231 141000
Dusseldorf 0211 327000
Frankfurt 069 288791
Hamburg 040 371173
Hanover 0511 326919
Karlsruhe 0721 25968
Munich 089 2608224
Munster 0251 42272
Nuernberg 0911 245181
Stuttgart 0711 2261064
Wiesbaden 0611 302086

ITALY
Milan 2 86463532

LUXEMBOURG
Luxembourg 221 320

NETHERLANDS
Amsterdam 020 6228087
Arnhem 085 430250

Eindhoven 040 435022
Groningen 031 50185060
The Hague 070 3600540
Maastricht 043 250972
Rotterdam 010 4148535
Utrecht 030 313051

SPAIN
Barcelona 341 25490

SWITZERLAND
Basel 061 2619757
Bern 031 210696
Geneva (clothes only) 22 3113494
Geneva (home furnishings only) 22 3103048
Zurich 01 2211394

ASIA
HONG KONG SHOPS IN SHOPS
Seibu 852 801 7849
Sogo 852 891 1787

JAPAN
Ginza 03 3571 5011
Yagota 052 836 7086
Kichijoji 0422 21 1203
Jiyugaoka 03 3724 0051
Yokohama LMP 045 222 5308
Shibuya 03 3464 5011
Futako Tamagawa 03 3708 3151
Gifu Melsa 0582 66 3136
Fukuoka Tenjin 092 716 7415
Rokko Island 078 857 8119

JAPAN SHOPS IN SHOPS
TOKYO
Mitsukoshi Shinjuku 03 3225 7389
Mitsukoshi Nihonbashi 03 3241 5617
Mitsukoshi Ikebukuro 03 3987 6074
Tokyu 03 3477 3836
Keio Shinjuku 03 3344 0080
Mitsukoshi Ginza 03 3561 4050
Tobu Ikebukuro 03 3980 0041

REST OF JAPAN
Mitsukoshi Yokohama 045 323 1683

Yokohama Prince Hotel 045 754 4655
Saikaya Kawasaki 0044 211 8581
Saikaya Yokosuka 0468 23 1234
Chiba Mitsukoshi 043 227 4731
Mitsukoshi Bandai 025 243 6333
Sapporo Tokyu 011 212 2658
Kintetsu Abeno 06 625 2332
Hankyu Umeda 06 365 0793
Kawanashi Hankyu 0727 56 1622
Mitsukoshi Hiroshima 082 241 5055
Hiroshima Sogo 082 225 2955
Hakata Izutsuya 092 452 2181
Fukuoka Tamaya 092 271 6588
Nagoya Mitsukoshi 052 252 1838
Matsuzakaya Nagoyacki 052 565 4339
Seishin Sogo 078 992 1586
Kobe Ilankyu 078 360 7528
Daimaru Kobe 078 333 4079
Tama Sogo 0423 39 2450
Kintetsu Kyoto 075 365 8024/8013
Be Me Machida Daimaru 0427 24 8174

Sanyo Himeji 0792 23 4792
Tenmaya Fukuyama 0849 27 2214
Mitsukoshi Matsuyama 0899 46 4829
Saikaya Fujisawa 0466 27 1111
Matsuzukaya Yokkaichi 0593 551241
Cita Tokiwa 0975 33 1741
Bon Belta Narita 0476 23 3236
Bon Belta Isojin Mito 0292 28 1185
Hanamatsu Matsubishi 053 452 2941
Kagoshima Mitsukoshi 0992 39 4635
Saga Tamaya 0952 28 0608
Kintetsu Nara 0742 30 2751

SINGAPORE SHOPS IN SHOPS
Sogo 65 334 1014
Isetan Scotts 65 735 0495

TAIWAN SHOPS IN SHOPS
Ta-Lee Isetan 886 7 241 8860
Pacific Sogo 886 2 740 9662
Shin Kong Mitsukoshi 886 2 382 4859

ACKNOWLEDGEMENTS

The publishers would like to thank the following photographers and organizations for their kind permission to reproduce the photographs in this book: 7 Ken Kirkwood; 8-9 Camera Press; 11 Ken Kirkwood; 12 Pia Tryde/Homes & Gardens/Robert Harding; 13 Lucinda Lambton/Arcaid; 48 Marie Claire Maison/ Christophe Dugied/ J. Postic; 62 Camron Public Relations; 63 Tom Leighton/Camera Press; 87 Jan Baldwin/ Homes & Gardens/Robert Harding; 88 Richard Bryant/Arcaid; 89 Fritz von der Schulenburg/The Interior World; 104 Camera Press; 117 Elizabeth Whitting Associates; 137 Camera Press.

The following photographs were taken especially for Laura Ashley/Ebury Press by Tim Imrie: 15, 16, 18, 21-3, 25-6, 29, 34-5, 40, 43, 47, 51, 52-5, 57, 59, 61, 66-7, 68, 75-6, 79, 82, 85-6, 90-91, 98-100, 103, 106-7, 108-110, 113-14, 116, 120-1, 125-7, 131, 133 and 136. Any photographs not included in this list belong to the Laura Ashley archive.

The publishers would also like to thank the following: The Blue Door (0181-748 9785), Crucial Trading (0171-221 9000), VV Rouleaux (0171-371 5929), Grant and Cutler (0171-498 6974), Artisan (0171-498 6974), C.P. Hart & Sons (0171-928 9660), Decorative Living (0171-736 5623), Cath Kidston (0171-221 4000), The Dining Room Shop (0181-878 1020), Joss Graham (0171-730 4370), Graham & Greene (0171-727 4594), David Wainwright (0171-792 1988) and Sacha Waddell (0171-385 6430).